# Images of the
# BLUES

# Images of the
# BLUES

## Lee Tanner
## Lee Hildebrand

*with a foreword by*
*David Ritz*

**FRIEDMAN/FAIRFAX**
PUBLISHERS

**A FRIEDMAN/FAIRFAX BOOK**

Library of Congress Cataloging-in-Publication data available on request.

ISBN 1-56799-693-0

Editors: Ann Kirby and Nathaniel Marunas
Art Director: Jeff Batzli
Photography Editor: Christopher C. Bain
Production Manager: Susan Kowal

Color separations by Colourscan
Printed in Hong Kong by Sing Cheong Printing

10 9 8 7 6 5 4 3 2 1

For bulk purchases and special sales, please contact:
Friedman/Fairfax Publishers
Attention: Sales Department
15 West 26th Street
New York, New York 10010
212/685-6610   FAX 212/685-1307

Visit our website:
http://www.metrobooks.com

**PAGE ONE: Joe Lewis Walker**
**FRONTPIECE: Buddy Guy**

## DEDICATIONS

For Louis Armstrong and Sidney Bechet, who prepared me for the whole world of the blues; and for Linda, my partner, my companion, my inspiration, and the love of my life.

—Lee Tanner

To the memory of the music and magic of Johnny Heartsman, and to my wife Connie for her continuing love and support.

—Lee Hildebrand

## ACKNOWLEDGEMENTS

Special thanks to the designer and the editors—Jeff Batzli, Ann Kirby, Sharyn Rosart, Nathaniel Marunas, Loretta Mowat, and Chris Bain—for their superb handling of the material. Special thanks to Helen Johnson, who keeps the wheels turning and all the lines of communication open, always with a delightful sense of humor. Finally, to John Turner, with deep appreciation for his expertise in all matters photographic.

**Paul Butterfield,
Cambridge, Massachusetts**

# Photographs
# Contributed by:

RAY AVERY

ESMOND EDWARDS

RAEBURN FLERLAGE

WILLIAM GOTTLIEB

STEPHEN GREEN

JEAN-PIERRE LELOIR

ROGER MARSHUTZ

ROBERT PARENT

JAN PERSSON

CHARLES PETERSON

JOSEPH A. ROSEN

EBET ROBERTS

DON SCHLITTEN

HERB SNITZER

LISA TANNER

LEE TANNER

MICHELLE VIGNES

VAL WILMER

AND THE FRANK DRIGGS
   COLLECTION

**Tampa Red.
Englewood, New Jersey,
1961**

# CONTENTS

A gathering of blues legends outside
of Rudy Van Gelder's recording studio.
Englewood Cliffs, N.J., 1961

1. Willie "The Lion" Smith, *pianist*

2. Cecil Scott, *saxophonist*

3. Victoria Spivey, *singer*

4. J.C. Higginbotham, *trombonist*

5. Sidney DeParis, *trumpeter*

6. Alberta Hunter, *singer*

7. Gene Brooks, *pianist*

8. Buster Bailey, *clarinetist*

9. Jimmy Rushing, *singer*

10. Henry Goodwin, *trumpeter*

11. Lucille Hegamin, *singer*

12. Zutty Singleton, *drummer*

# FOREWORD: SEEING THE BLUES

I HEARD THE BLUES BEFORE I SAW THEM. AND I HAD THE BLUES before I knew them because they were all around me. Yet the blues didn't have faces. So to see those faces—T-Bone's flashing smile, Wolf's raging grimace, the sweetness of Muddy's eyes—was a revelation and a shock. The faces that made the blues—the faces that *were* the blues—held a fascination and an allure as compelling as the music itself.

The blues are deeply visual. We experience them as pictures. When Joe Turner sings, "You wear those dresses, the sun comes shining through....I can't believe my eyes, all that mess belongs to you," no accompanying illustration is required. But beyond being visual, the blues are downright visionary, painting an emotional landscape the size of Dante's *Divine Comedy*. The blues are the music of the human soul—raw, real, and lit by the light of honest expression. "The blues are simple music, and I'm a simple man," B.B. King told me when I began cowriting his autobiography in 1995. "But the blues aren't a science; the blues can't be broken down like mathematics. The blues are a mystery, and mysteries are never as simple as they look."

So we search for clues. We seek out the bluesmen and -women. We study their stories and their faces, and listening to their songs over and over again, we search their eyes for the secrets of their sound. Lee Tanner's wonderful collection of blues portraits is full of such searches and secrets. It is a book as seductive as the silent soundtrack that runs beneath its pictures. It is essential. It is a view of the blues that excites the mind.

When, for example, I view Tanner's clear-eyed study of John Lee Hooker, I remember my own first glimpse of the man himself. Hooker's "Boogie Chillen" had fired my imagination, but I didn't know what real-life image to expect when I walked into a smokey Austin roadhouse in the prehippie sixties to find a man free of pretenses, fancy clothes, and traditional rhymes. The great free-verse bluesman played sitting down, just as he sits in Tanner's shot, a monument of ferocious grace.

Grace is the quality, the paradox, the element that gives the blues and its masters such visceral appeal. Grace and grit. This book is replete with such glorious pictures: in Stephen Green's lyrical rendering, Etta James, a woman of great physical and emotional power, spreads her arms as she readies to sail into heavenly spheres. And in Tanner's take on the young Aretha, we see a singer caught in the act of catharsis. The images say what our hearts are thinking: that the blues transform, turning common pain into uncommon poetry.

Lee Hildebrand's informed text also says what true blues lovers have long known: the form is varied and wondrously complex; as a category, the blues defy neat categorization. The spillover from the California trio blues of Charles Brown to the country blues of Mance Lipscomb to the jazz blues of Billie Holiday to the gospel blues of Dinah Washington to the rhythm and blues of Hank Ballard is one engaging mess. It is all surprisingly different, all surprisingly same, all rooted in a rich soil whose blooms are perennial. In the author's happy phrase, we live in

**Jazz drummer and promoter Johnny Otis ran one of the great touring R&B shows that gave a vital break to many singers, like Little Esther and "Big Mama" Thornton. New York City, 1994**

"the blues century." For all their modesty, for all their deceptive and moving simplicity, the blues are omnipotent. They define our time.

The time for the blues is yesterday and today. Because the blues carry hidden codes of past conditions—personal, political, and sexual—they carry historical weight. They have cultural substance. But because those conditions are so basic to human nature, history is renewed every time a blues is played. Every true blues is a new blues, an echo of a blues once heard and the template for fresh blues to come. No music is more self-referring, yet no music is less self-conscious.

I love the crosscurrents of the blues, another phenomenon caught so beautifully by these photographs. Johnny Otis, a great blues practitioner and promoter, once told me, "Max Roach and Lightnin' Hopkins aren't just like first cousins; they're blood brothers." Their common blood is the blues.

When I was young and naive, I sought a strict definition of the blues. When I interviewed Thelonious Monk, I asked him to provide me one. The brilliant bebopper sat for several minutes, studied the floor, and didn't say a word. Finally he went to the piano and played a few simple blues licks before leaving the room without uttering a word.

Charles Brown, the world's most charming blues exponent, tried to accommodate me. "It's hard to put it in words," he said. "It's just a certain kind of picture some people can paint."

When I asked bluesman Jimmy Reed, he groaned under his breath before setting me straight. "It ain't about words," he explained. "Just look at me when I'm playing. Look how I blow my harp; look how I stroke my guitar. Man, just look."

I can't say it any better.

Just look.

*David Ritz*

# INTRODUCTION

I WAS STEEPED IN THE BLUES FROM THE MOMENT I DISCOVERED jazz in Boston in the late 1930s. Instrumental blues were played to perfection by the Basie, Ellington, Erskine Hawkins, and Earl Hines bands. The great soloists Louis Armstrong, Roy Eldridge, Sidney Bechet, as well as Charlie Christian and Cootie Williams with Benny Goodman's sextet, provided memorable performances both on the radio and during live stage shows. Williams, a particular favorite of mine, went on to form an excellent band of his own, which, incidentally, was the first to feature the music of Thelonious Monk. When they first played the RKO Boston theater, I was treated to a startling tour-de-force by lanky, bald-headed saxophonist Eddie Vinson, who played and sang the blues like nobody I'd ever heard before. Known as "Mr. Cleanhead," his featured

**FAR RIGHT:**
**Blues shouter and saxist Eddie "Cleanhead" Vinson preparing his trademark bald head before a 1974 festival appearance in Berlin.**

**RIGHT:**
**Guitarist Charlie Christian (right) with Benny Goodman and producer John Hammond (left) at a 1940 Columbia recording session.**

solo spot was a raunchy tune called "Cherry Red." He opened it with a searing blast of phrases on his alto and then he shouted out the blues with a rich, deep, gravely voice. When he was finished, he cradled the alto in his arms like a baby and casually drifted off stage right, while Cootie and the band tore their way into the tune. Just when it seemed time for a reprise, "Cleanhead" drifted back to the microphone, this time from stage left, and proceeded to blow us away once again. What an experience for a teenager...drama at its best.

Singer-guitarist Teddy Bunn made several memorable Blue Note recordings in 1940 with The Port of Harlem Jazzmen, which included Frankie Newton (shown here), as well as Sidney Bechet, Sid Catlett, and J.C. Higginbotham.

But this was only one piece of the blues. It wasn't until the late 1950s that I started listening seriously to the rest of the broad blues spectrum. On the one hand, the intriguing material written, played, and sung by jazz pianist Mose Allison, along with my interest in folk music, directed me to southern rural blues. On the other, the music of British blues-rockers led me to the urban blues of Chicago. My appreciation of the blues broadened to include the work of Muddy Waters, John Lee Hooker, Mississippi John Hurt, Albert King, Junior Wells, B.B. King, and many more. The musicianship and the singing of these performers struck me as remarkable, and since then I have cherished the work of diverse talents, from Buddy Guy and Jimi Hendrix, to such greats as Joe Louis Walker and Robben Ford.

When I finished putting together my prints for the book *Images of Jazz*, I knew I wanted to do a similar book on the blues. However, I faced two hurdles. First, I did not have quite enough images on my own to do a representative presentation, and second, I was not knowledgeable enough about this subject to write the accompanying text. I solved the first problem by finding superb blues images by several excellent photographers, some of whom I knew (including my daughter Lisa) and some whom I discovered for the first time. The text I put into the capable hands of blues and jazz critic/historian Lee Hildebrand. The result of our cooperative venture lies in the pages before you.

*Lee Tanner*

# The Blues Century

No one knows for sure precisely when or where the blues were first sung and played—sometime around the turn of the twentieth century is the most common estimate—or even how the name "blues" was given to this uniquely American form of music. It is a fact, however, that by the 1920s, when the first recordings of blues were made, blues had become an important force in the cultural life of the United States. Blues had a vast influence on the development of other musical forms, especially jazz, gospel, and country music. In 1949, blues with a heavy beat was tagged "rhythm and blues." Two years later, the label "rock and roll" was applied, and blues-based music swiftly swept the world. By the 1990s, pure blues forms no longer enjoyed a wide degree of popularity—despite a significant resurgence of interest from some quarters—yet the influence of blues can still be felt in jazz, gospel, country, rock, soul, and hip-hop.

Contrary to a belief held by some, blues music did not come directly out of Africa. It was created in the southern part of the United States during the latter part of the nineteenth century by the still-suffering children of Africans who had been brought to North American shores in chains. While toiling long days in the fields, slaves devised hollers and work songs with call-and-response patterns to communicate and to help pass the hours of backbreaking labor. Similar call-and-response singing patterns were common to the cultural traditions of many western African cultures, from which a large portion of these slaves came. Stripped of their religious customs, slaves were forced to adopt Christianity, which their masters hoped would keep them subservient with its promise of an afterlife. Instead, it provided them an outlet through which to express their pain. In their worship, they created spirituals, many with subtle messages of protest against their oppression. Both the field hollers and the spirituals were important precursors to the blues. While Africa can be pointed to as a distant source for the vocal inflections and sliding notes used in the blues, the unique three-chord sequence utilized in most blues songs cannot be found in any previous form of music.

Blues is generally a vocal music, although it can be performed by instrumentalists alone. The blues melody is based on a scale in which the third, fifth, seventh, and sometimes sixth degrees are casually flattened. At these degrees, the performer is likely to slide into the notes, creating what are called blue notes. A blues singer frequently employs such vocal devices as falsetto, shouting, whining, moaning, and growling, all of which can be traced back to African traditions.

> ...the blackfolk of America. Unsung they sing. Or they play a musical instrument. Despite the permanent trauma of poverty and an almost ubiquitous sadness, there is gaiety....But if it is "happiness," the term can only be rendered in the religiously ecstatic sense of "Divine" as conceived in the West African spirit. This oneness of the spirit is aptly displayed in the title of the gospel song "Happy Am I" made popular by the Elder Lightfoot and often quoted by Charlie Parker in his blues renditions. It is a happiness that transcends mere laughter. It is a Yoruba happiness, a total affirmation.
>
> —Archie Shepp,
> **musician and educator**

Ma Rainey, the "Mother of the Blues," seen here with her Georgia Band, was one of the most influential of the female blues artists.

A specific sequence of chords is used to accompany a typical twelve-bar blues song. The first four-measure line is supported by a tonic chord (a chord built on the first degree of the scale). The second four-measure line is accompanied by a subdominant chord (a chord built on the fourth degree) for two measures, followed by a return to the tonic for the next two measures. The third line employs a dominant chord (a chord built on the fifth degree) for two measures, then resolves in the tonic for the final two. Related chords are sometimes substituted during the performance of a twelve-bar blues.

Blues lyrics can express a wide range of human emotions and concerns, including jubilation and despair, and can have a cathartic effect on both performer and listener. Most blues songs are made up of three or more verses of twelve measures each, with each verse divided into sections of four measures. The first line is sung twice, followed by a rhymed response. A statement is made, repeated, and answered. Because each line of the lyric does not fill up the entire four-bar space over which it is sung, the remaining space is completed by an instrumental response, most commonly played by a guitarist, although instrumental backing for a blues singer can range from a single guitarist or pianist to a band of any size.

The first known blues singers were men who sang and played guitar at dances, picnics, and other social functions. Many performed on the streets of cities and towns through which they traveled, with tips from passersby as the only compensation.

**Bessie Smith's magnificent voice could make a work of art out of even the dreariest pop song.**

Some, such as Blind Lemon Jefferson (from Texas) and Blind Willie McTell (from Georgia), were blind men who found music the only way to make a living in a time before the government began providing assistance to disabled persons. Besides Jefferson and McTell, such other guitar-toting bluesmen as Peg Leg Howell and Barbecue Bob (both from Georgia) and Charley Patton (from Mississippi) made successful recordings of rural, or "country," blues during the latter part of the 1920s. Their records were bought almost entirely by African-Americans, and their music was all but unknown to whites, except for a few (like Jimmie Rodgers, known as "the Blue Yodeler," a singer-guitarist from Mississippi who helped lay the foundations of modern country music by adding four-measure yodeling sections to twelve-bar blues).

Even more successful than the bluesmen of the 1920s were the women who performed in a style known as classic blues. Gertrude "Ma" Rainey (from Georgia) and her disciple, Bessie Smith (from Tennessee), were the queens of classic blues. They were big-voiced women who sang in vaudeville theaters throughout the southern and northern states, appearing in shows with comedians, dancers, jugglers, and other variety acts. In person and on record, the classic blues singers were often accompanied by top jazz musicians, including trumpeters Louis Armstrong, Tommy Ladnier, and King Oliver; clarinetists Buster Bailey and Johnny Dodds; saxophonists Sidney Bechet and Coleman Hawkins; and pianists Fletcher Henderson and Jelly Roll Morton. As Bessie Smith once put it, she "used only high-class musicians" for her shows. Besides Ma Rainey and Bessie Smith, other important blueswomen of the 1920s included Ida Cox, Alberta Hunter, Lillian Glenn (or Glinn), Lucille Hegamin, Mamie Smith, Bertha "Chippie" Hill, Margaret Johnson, Trixie Smith, Victoria Spivey, Beulah "Sippie" Wallace, Ethel Waters, Clara Smith, and Edith Wilson. After the 1920s, women no longer dominated the blues, although such women as Big Maybelle, Ruth Brown, Lil Green, Helen Humes, Denise LaSalle, Memphis Minnie, Little Esther Phillips, Koko Taylor, Willie Mae "Big Mama" Thornton, and Dinah Washington had successful careers as blues singers in subsequent years.

The ragtime-spiced picking of such guitarists from the southeastern states as Blind Blake, Blind Willie McTell, Gary Davis, Blind Boy Fuller, and Brownie McGhee had considerable impact during the pre–World War II blues era, but it was the musicians from Mississippi and Texas who cast a more lasting shadow over the development of the blues.

The early Mississippi country blues style is associated with such artists as Charley Patton, Son House, Skip James, Tommy Johnson, John Hurt, Bukka White, and Robert Johnson (whose alleged deal with the devil and still-not-entirely-solved murder have taken on mythical proportions over the years). Patton, House, James, White, and Robert Johnson were masters of the bottleneck guitar who produced a shimmering metallic sound by running the broken-off neck of a glass bottle over the strings on the instrument's fretboard with one hand while picking the strings with the other. This raw, searing style was brought north after the war by Muddy Waters and Elmore James, who made it even more intense through the use of amplification.

The early Texas country blues guitarists, of which Blind Lemon Jefferson was the most popular and influential, seldom used bottlenecks. They instead fretted with their fingers to produce fast single-note runs. Aaron "T-Bone" Walker was the first to play Texas blues on an electric guitar, and his innovations had a vast influence on other guitar players. Texas country blues, however, continued to be popular into the postwar era through the work of Lightnin' Hopkins, Lil' Son Jackson, and Smokey Hogg.

The blues, which was born in the South, took hold in the North during the 1920s, especially in such cities as Chicago, St. Louis, and Indianapolis. Pianist Leroy Carr and his partner, guitarist Scrapper Blackwell, were instrumental in creating a smoother, more urban style of blues. Another variation on the blues was boogie-woogie, a fast, romping piano style built around an eight-notes-to-the-measure bass figure played with the left hand. Pinetop Smith first popularized boogie-woogie in the late 1920s, but the style became a national craze a decade later through the work of pianists Albert Ammons, Pete Johnson, and Meade "Lux" Lewis. Other important city blues musicians of the 1920s and 1930s included singer-guitarists Lonnie Johnson, Big Bill Broonzy, and Tampa Red; singer-pianists Walter Davis, Big Maceo Merriweather, and Peetie Wheatstraw; and singer-harmonica player John Lee "Sonny Boy" Williamson.

Although blues and jazz had moved in different directions by the end of the 1920s, some blues singers continued working with jazz bands, Jimmy Rushing and Helen Humes with the Count Basie Orchestra and Walter Brown with Jay McShann being among the most

famous. (Billie Holiday, Ella Fitzgerald, and other band vocalists also sang occasional blues as part of their popular-song repertoires, but their phrasing owed more to the jazz vocal tradition of Louis Armstrong than to classic or country blues.) Joe Turner, who shouted the blues with world-class jazz players from the 1930s into the 1980s, and singer-saxophonist Louis Jordan, who performed humorous up-tempo blues with a pronounced backbeat (in which the second and fourth beats of each measure of 4/4 time are accented on a snare drum), pioneered a style during the 1940s that became known as rhythm and blues at the end of that decade.

While the searing electric bottleneck and amplified harmonica sounds rooted in Mississippi country blues formed the basis of the eclectic postwar Memphis and Chicago styles of artists like Howlin' Wolf, Little Junior Parker, Muddy Waters, and Little Walter, Texas-hewn styles took on new dimensions

**Blind Lemon Jefferson was a giant during his time, as well as a commercial success.**

after being transplanted to Los Angeles and Oakland. Texas-born pianists Ivory Joe Hunter, Charles Brown, Lloyd Glenn, Amos Milburn, Floyd Dixon, and Little Willie Littlefield created a new California blues style that was part jazz and part boogie-woogie. Inspired by Louis Jordan, southern California bandleaders Roy Milton, Joe Liggins, and Johnny Otis developed a rocking blues combo style that some called jump blues. And T-Bone Walker had a pronounced influence on such young California blues guitarists as Lowell Fulson, Pee Wee Crayton, Lafayette Thomas, Pete Lewis, Jimmy Nolen, and Johnny Heartsman.

In Memphis during the late 1940s, singer-guitarist B.B. King made a radical leap forward in the way the blues guitar is played. Unable to master the bottleneck style of his native Mississippi, he created a similar sound by turning the volume of his amplifier up high and moving his left hand rapidly as he held one finger in place on the fretboard. This technique allowed notes to ring out at high volume, often being sustained over several measures. Much like New Orleans blues belter Roy Brown, King sang in a wailing falsetto derived from gospel music. Both as a guitarist and as a vocalist, King became the most influential bluesman of the postwar era, inspiring other blues artists such as Albert King, Bobby Bland, Little Milton, Otis Rush, Freddie King, Buddy Guy, and Little Joe Blue, as well as such rock guitarists as Eric Clapton, Jeff Beck, Jimi Hendrix, Carlos Santana, and the artist who once called himself Prince.

By the mid-1950s, blues with a strong backbeat had captured the world's imagination. Not only had rhythm and blues and rock and roll taken hold in the black community, but increasing numbers of young whites were showing interest in what to them was a new musical style that had a vitality missing in much white popular music of the period. Many in the first

**Big Bill Broonzy in a studio pose with his elegant Gibson cutaway scroll guitar.**

generation of rock and roll stars, including Joe Turner, Ruth Brown, Fats Domino, Chuck Berry, Bo Diddley, and Ray Charles, were African-American. Charles, a blind Florida-born pianist and singer, was the most innovative, having developed a new style (which some called "soul") that fused the cool jazz and blues of Nat "King" Cole and Charles Brown; the hot, emotionally charged gospel sounds of Alex Bradford and others; and even a touch of country music. The first white singer to have a rock and roll hit was Bill Haley, who based his style in part on those of Joe Turner and Louis Jordan. Haley's popularity was small in comparison to that of Mississippi-born, Memphis-based truck driver Elvis Presley, who developed an energetic form of rock and roll drawn from the blues of Roy Brown, Arthur Crudup, and Little Junior Parker, as well as from white gospel, country, and pop styles. By 1956, Presley was unquestionably the most popular entertainer in the world.

Presley's unprecedented popularity did not lead large numbers of white people to the blues, perhaps because the overt blues content of his repertoire was too small to inspire a groundswell. During the 1960s, however, white blues groups began to emerge for the first time, including the Blues Project and the Butterfield Blues Band (both in the United States) and John Mayall's Bluesbreakers and Fleetwood Mac (both in England). The success of these bands created a lasting white fan base for blues music. Young white blues fans embraced some, though not all, of the genre's black stars. B.B. King and Albert King, who had inspired new guitar "gods" Michael Bloomfield (of the Butterfield Blues Band and the Electric Flag) and Eric Clapton (of the Bluesbreakers and Cream), were afforded elder statesman status, while such others as Bobby Bland and Lowell Fulson, whose influence on white blues was negligible, were largely ignored.

A new form of gospel-imbued blues singing emerged during the 1950s and 1960s through the work of such soul-blues artists as Little Willie John, Ted Taylor, Johnnie Taylor, Little Johnny Taylor, and Little Milton. With the exception of Milton, who played guitar during part of his performances, none of these vocalists played instruments. By the mid-1990s, Bland, Johnnie Taylor, and Milton, along with Denise LaSalle, were the most popular blues attractions in African-American communities across the United States, regularly appearing at large clubs and auditoriums along what was left of the so-called chitlin circuit, yet they were seldom invited to perform at the clubs and festivals to which white blues fans flocked.

Jimmy McCracklin, an Oakland-based blues singer, pianist, and songwriter who had a string of rhythm and blues hits between 1958 and 1966, has complained about record companies who assign white engineers to mix down his tunes to two-track stereo from multitrack session tapes. White engineers, McCracklin contended, tend to focus on the instruments over the vocals, whereas black engineers put the vocals in the foreground. It is the lyrics, he stressed, that sell a song, particularly to African-American record buyers; if they're lost in the mix, the record is doomed.

Herein lies the crux of racial segregation that continues to poison the blues world. To African-Americans, the blues is first and foremost a vocal music. Singers are the true stars of the blues, and instrumental solos are kept relatively brief. (Don Robey, one of the few black men who produced blues hits during the 1950s and 1960s, often truncated harmonica solos on Junior Parker records and guitar solos on Bobby Bland records to four bars instead of the normal twelve.) To whites raised on rock, instrumental ability is all-important, far outweighing vocal style. Long solos are the rule, and guitar hotshots like Johnny Winter and Stevie Ray Vaughan, neither of whom was much of a singer, rule the roost.

Ruth Brown and other rhythm and blues artists who toured the South during the 1950s—when laws strictly prohibited blacks and whites from mixing in schools, libraries, hotels, theaters, nightclubs, restaurants, rest rooms, and swimming pools, at drinking fountains, on beaches and public transportation, and on and on, ad nauseam—tell of dances at which ropes were strung down the middle of auditoriums to separate black and white members of the audiences from one another. Sometimes, however, the ropes would drop to the floor and the dancers would mingle.

Such laws no longer exist, yet as the blues prepares to enter the next century, its black and white constituencies are largely divided, as if the ropes were still in place.

"How long?" Leroy Carr cried out in 1928, and still there is no answer in sight.

# T-Bone Walker

AARON THIBEAUX WALKER (1913–1975) WAS ONE OF THE giants of American music, a true innovator whose influence was all-pervasive. T-Bone, as he was known professionally, ranks with Louis Armstrong, Coleman Hawkins, Charlie Christian, Jimmy Blanton, Little Walter, Clifton Chenier, and very few others as a musician who single-handedly created an instrumental style that affected, either directly or indirectly, that of virtually every other player of his instrument who came after him. There hasn't been an electric guitarist who has played blues or rock over the past half century who has escaped Walker's influence. The list includes B.B. King, Lowell Fulson, Pee Wee Crayton, Freddie King, Clarence "Gatemouth" Brown, Johnny "Guitar" Watson, Albert Collins, Chuck Berry, Jimmy Nolen, Albert King, Jimi Hendrix, Eric Clapton, Jeff Beck, Jimmy Page, Keith Richards, Stevie Ray Vaughan, Robert Cray, and Duke Robillard.

"T-Bone Walker is the fundamental source of the modern blues style of playing and singing the blues," blues historian Pete Welding once stated, "and is widely regarded as having started it all back in the late 1930s when, almost alone, he forged the fleet, jazz-based guitar style that has since become the dominant approach for the instrument and, with it, the blues itself. In a very real sense the modern blues is largely his creation. The blues was different before he came onto the scene and it hasn't been the same since, and few men can lay claim to that kind of

> T-Bone Walker has a touch that nobody has been able to duplicate. I've tried my best to get that sound, especially in the late 1940s and early 1950s. I came pretty close, but never quite got it.
> —B.B. King

distinction; real talent is uncommon enough but genius is rarer still."

Although Walker could hold his own among the very finest of jazz musicians—Lester Young, Teddy Wilson, and Dizzy Gillespie among them—he was primarily identified with blues and was thus given scant attention by critics during and after his lifetime. His records were sold almost exclusively to black people, and because his best work was recorded prior to the advent of rock and roll, he never crossed over to the pop market during the mid-1950s as did Joe Turner, Fats Domino, and several other blues artists. By the second blues crossover period, (mid-1960s) when the popularity of the Rolling Stones, John Mayall, and the Butterfield Blues Band led another generation of whites to discover the blues, Walker was in decline both musically and physically, and thus enjoyed little of the notoriety that was afforded such other bluesmen as B.B. King, Muddy Waters, Albert King, and Howlin' Wolf.

Walker never even enjoyed the full fruits of his labor. He recorded his most famous composition, the blues standard "Call It Stormy Monday," in 1947. "I haven't never had but one big hit, and it's bigger than 'St. Louis Blues,'" he told Jim and Amy O'Neal two and a half years before his death. "Everybody's playing it.

fussed a lot with the musicians, frequently stopping mid-solo to motion with his hands for them to play softer.

During the summer of 1966, a night or two after one of Walker's ill-fated juke joint performances in nearby North Richmond, he turned up at the Oakland Coliseum Arena as an unadvertised guest on promoter Norman Granz's final Jazz at the Philharmonic tour. The bill was amazing: Duke Ellington and His Orchestra, Ella Fitzgerald with the Tommy Flanagan Trio and Roy Eldridge, the Oscar Peterson Trio, and soloists Zoot Sims, Clark Terry, and, in one of his final public appearances, Coleman Hawkins. "The Father of the Tenor Saxophone," as Hawkins was often called, gave the kind of performance audiences had come to expect of Walker. Frail and sporting an unkempt beard, Hawkins began his solo spot with a ballad, backed by the Peterson trio. Hawkins' tone was harsh and his phrasing pained, and midway through the tune he let out an excruciating wail through his horn, stopped playing, and began weaving in place. Peterson got up from the piano, braced Hawkins, and escorted him offstage.

After Terry and Ellington sidemen Johnny Hodges and Paul Gonsalves did their showcase numbers, emcee Granz came out and announced, "Ladies and gentlemen, we have a surprise for you tonight—the great T-Bone Walker." Terry, Hodges, Gonsalves, and the Peterson trio joined him in two slow blues—"Woman, You Must Be Crazy" and his famous "Call It Stormy Monday." He appeared sober, and his vocals were nearly as strong and his playing almost as fluid as on his old records. Walker had risen to the occasion, no doubt because Granz, unlike the bookers at the ghetto clubs where Walker had grown accustomed to working, had provided him with musicians of a caliber equal to his own. Granz had given Walker respect, and Walker gave it back.

More and more are playing it now, and everybody knows about it, which is good. But I'm still not getting my money." The problem was that most recorded versions of the song, including Bobby Bland's 1962 hit, were mistakenly titled "Stormy Monday Blues," which was an earlier and totally different composition by Earl Hines and Billy Eckstine, who ended up receiving both the label credit and the royalties.

Born in Linden, Texas, and raised in the Oak Cliff section of Dallas, Walker was an undisciplined youth who took to drinking and gambling as a teenager. In 1955, ulcers forced the removal of two-thirds of his stomach, though he continued drinking heavily.

Walker spent much of his final decade performing in relative obscurity on the West Coast, often at neighborhood bars in the San Francisco Bay/Oakland area. The house rhythm sections were generally second-rate and Walker was usually drunk, unable to play with his guitar behind his head, let alone do the splits that had made him such a showstopping entertainer during the 1940s and 1950s. He fumbled a lot on his guitar and

T-BONE WALKER

A T-Bone offspring, Johnny "Guitar" Watson
was one of the first blues artists to use
amplifier reverb effects.
Paris, 1980

"[Clarence
'Gatemouth' Brown's
1947] impromptu fill-
in for an ailing T-Bone
Walker in a Houston
nightclub boosted
Brown's career."
(Bill Dahl, writer)
Chicago, 1988

# JOE TURNER

It was obvious to anyone who witnessed a performance by Joe Turner (1911–1985) during the last decade of his life that the great Kansas City blues shouter was not a well man. He would amble slowly to the stage as he supported his rotund frame with a cane, sit down on a stool, and tap the cane vigorously on the floor to indicate the desired tempo to whatever pickup band was on hand for the evening. Then he'd open his mouth and the blues would pour out in a majestic baritone seemingly unaffected by all the years of hard living. Regardless of whether his enunciation occasionally faltered due to dental problems, his timing was perfect and his choice of notes that of a master musician. Singing chorus after twelve-bar chorus, many plucked off the top of his head and nearly all in the key of C, Turner would transport himself and his audience to a place where trouble no longer occupied the forefront of the mind. "As soon as he came on stage, the lights went on again," said Eric Miller, producer of some of Turner's final recordings.

During a prolific career that lasted nearly half a century, Turner recorded with a wide variety of instrumental accompanists—from such well-schooled jazzmen as Art Tatum, Coleman Hawkins, and Dizzy Gillespie to intuitive blues players like Elmore James and Pee Wee Crayton—but he never bent his brassy, rhythmically riveting style to match theirs. He was "the Boss of the Blues," and they followed his lead. From such early recordings with pianist Pete Johnson as "Roll 'em Pete" and "Piney Brown Blues" to rock and roll hits of the mid-1950s like "Honey Hush," "Shake, Rattle, and Roll," and "Corrine Corrina,"

Turner's surefooted vocal delivery never changed. As bandleader Johnny Otis once stated, "He went from 'Piney Brown Blues' to 'Shake, Rattle, and Roll' without dropping a beat."

Besides singing spirituals in church, Turner grew up belting the blues on street corners, often accompanied by blind guitarists whom he led about. While in his mid-teens, he worked as a cook, waiter, bartender, and bouncer at Kansas City nightclubs.

At Piney Brown's Sunset Cafe during the 1930s, Turner shouted the blues from behind the bar while pouring drinks as Pete Johnson and such saxophone greats as Ben Webster, Lester Young, and Charlie Parker played from the bandstand. A public-address system was installed so that Turner's cavernous tones would carry out onto the street and attract customers into the bar. "People used to say they could hear me hollerin' five blocks away," the singer told journalist Mark Humphrey.

Turner's career as a singing bartender blossomed, as did Kansas City nightlife in general, in a wide-open atmosphere overseen by the corrupt Mayor Tom Pendergast. The good times came to an end, however, with a crackdown that followed Pendergast's 1938 conviction for income tax evasion.

> I've been doing that stuff they call rock-and-roll all along. I was doing it in Kansas City at the Sunset Club, back in the 1930s. There were country people around, singing those slo-o-ow blues, but I wanted to put that rhythm to it. Nobody sang the blues with rhythm like that before me.
> —Joe Turner

OPPOSITE:
Joe Turner said, "I just sing what pops into my mind. I don't plan nothing. I have no plans. I live my whole life in music, and I don't tell nobody my secrets."
New York City, 1983

Fortunately for Turner and pianist Johnson, their careers really took off in New York City that year. Producer John Hammond sent for the duo to perform in his now legendary Spirituals to Swing concert at Carnegie Hall. They then made a guest appearance on Benny Goodman's *Camel Caravan* program on CBS Radio, signed with Vocalion Records, and became the toast of Barney Josephson's two prestigious Cafe Society clubs, where they were often teamed with pianists Albert Ammons and Meade Lux Lewis as "the Boogie Woogie Boys." Turner and Johnson's Cafe Society gigs lasted more than four years.

Turner thrived in this new multiracial show business environment. "I had two cooks, one bottle washer, and one chauffeur," he bragged jokingly to author Peter Guralnick. "I had four cats to help me with my clothes on, help me with my clothes off, and help themselves to my money."

> Without changing his style or compromising his art in any way, Turner in the course of his career made his mark in the worlds of blues, jazz, rhythm-and-blues, and rock 'n' roll.
> —Peter Keepnews,
> **writer**

Although Turner continued having occasional hit records into the late 1940s, his fortunes were on the wane by 1950, when he appeared at the Apollo Theater with Count Basie's combo. Turner was having trouble adapting to the tight arrangements that had been written for his predecessor, Jimmy Rushing, and became so confused that the notoriously tough Harlem audience booed him. Ahmet Ertegun, co-owner of the fledgling Atlantic record label, was in attendance and found the singer at a neighborhood bar after the show. "I walked over to him and told him to pay no mind," the producer recalled, "that he really

wasn't a band singer anyway, but a great singer in his own right, and that I was going to record him and things would pick up for all of us."

Things most certainly did pick up: between 1951 and 1956, Turner scored fourteen top ten R&B hits for Atlantic, two of which—"Honey Hush" (an original Turner tune) and "Shake, Rattle, and Roll" (composed and arranged by Kansas City jazz veteran Jesse Stone)—went to number one on *Billboard's* R&B chart and made significant inroads onto the pop charts at a time when few rhythm and blues records were getting play on white-oriented stations. Turner, then in his forties, had become a teen idol of the early rock and roll era.

"I've been doing that stuff they call rock and roll all along," Turner once told an interviewer. "I was doing it in Kansas City at the Sunset Club, back in the 1930s. There were country people around, singing those slo-o-ow blues, but I wanted to put that rhythm to it. Nobody sang the blues with rhythm like that before me."

**ABOVE:**
**Turner recorded with preeminent tenor saxophonist Coleman Hawkins.**
**Boston, 1958**

**OPPOSITE:**
**Joe Turner worked with Count Basie (standing) on several occasions throughout his career.**
**Chicago, 1956**

ABOVE:

**Jimmy Rushing, a blues shouter like Turner, would often try to outshout the blaring Basie band, and this created an even more exciting performance.**

**"Joe [Williams] felt as if he hadn't really been singing the blues until he heard Turner sing and shout," wrote Leslie Gourse. Boston, 1968**

JOE TURNER

"We set the atmosphere, and you
couldn't be too loud. You had to
be mellow and play songs that set
the mood for the drinking,"
Charles Brown recalled.
Chicago, 1995

# Charles Brown

Charles Brown (b. 1921) might have become a major pop star, perhaps as big as his friend Nat "King" Cole, had market forces not conspired at the close of World War II to take the singer-pianist's career in a different direction. Brown was born in Texas City, Texas, and worked briefly as a high school teacher and chemist before relocating to Los Angeles in 1943. There he became a charter member of guitarist Johnny Moore's Three Blazers, a combo modeled on the King Cole Trio (in which Johnny's brother Oscar played guitar). The Three Blazers landed a gig at the posh Talk of the Town supper club in Beverly Hills, where their repertoire consisted of such pop tunes of the day as "My Silent Love," "There Is No Greater Love," and "How Deep Is the Ocean," jive numbers like "Hep Cats Gather Around," and a few jazzed-up versions of melodies by two of Brown's favorite composers—Franz Liszt and Claude Debussy. About the closest they got to blues was Brown's romping rendition of Earl Hines' "Boogie Woogie on the St. Louis Blues."

While the Three Blazers were entertaining white folks—with Brown flashing a toothy grin on the advice of the trio's agent—another young singer-pianist, the still-in-uniform Private Cecil Gant, was across town cutting a blues ballad titled "I Wonder" for Richard A. Nelson's upstart Gilt-Edge record label. In spite of its poor fidelity, a condition heightened by the fact that it was pressed on material that resembled asphalt, "I Wonder" became a massive seller in African-American communities throughout the country during the winter of 1944–1945. Gilt-Edge successfully filled a niche in the marketplace for "race music" that had been all but abandoned by the major companies due to wartime shellac shortages. Other shoestring record operations quickly sprung up, including Eddie Mesner's Philo label.

The Three Blazers signed with Philo, and for their first session for the company, in November 1945, Mesner wanted to hear a blues. Brown obliged with "Drifting Blues," a melancholy original composition he'd been doing with the Three Blazers when they performed for black audiences at after-hours joints like the Cobra Club ("out on First and San Pedro," he recalled, "where the black people took over the Japanese places"). The record, featuring Brown's breathy, brooding baritone voice and Texas piano triplets along with Moore's Charlie Christian–inspired guitar, became one of the major "race" hits of 1946 and established a stylistic course that Brown followed on subsequent sides with the Three Blazers and, after 1948, with his own blues groups.

Although largely unknown to the white public, hit songs like "New Orleans Blues," "Changeable Woman Blues," and "Merry Christmas Baby" made Brown the most popular blues artist in black America—so popular, in fact, that in 1947 Oscar Moore left Nat Cole, whose career was in full bloom, to join the Three Blazers. Brown remained a major record seller and attraction on the African-American

> Charles created a soft but very expressive style of blues which developed in the club atmosphere of Los Angeles in the late 1940s and early 1950s. This so-called club blues was a unique blend of the rough Texas blues tradition and the glamorous Hollywood atmosphere.
> —Per Notini, writer

theater circuit until 1952, when problems with the musicians' union and the IRS, coupled with his unwillingness to adapt his gentle musical approach to the rapidly emerging rock and roll style, began to derail his career. Elements of his sophisticated, jazz-informed approach to blues, however, continued to be felt in the music of such artists as Ray Charles, Fats Domino, Johnny Ace, Jesse Belvin, and Chuck Berry.

For the next three and a half decades, Brown existed on the periphery of show business, recording sporadically and performing in small clubs with often inadequate pickup bands, and even abandoning the piano for a long period in favor of the organ (which he played well but on which, unlike the piano, he did not project a signature style). He became a largely forgotten figure, remembered only at Christmastime when his two oft-covered seasonal hits, "Merry Christmas Baby"

and "Please Come Home for Christmas," filled the airwaves on black-oriented radio stations from coast to coast.

In 1984, Brown moved into a modest studio apartment in a senior citizens' home in Berkeley, California. There, he practiced Liszt and Debussy every morning before driving to nearby Golden Gate Fields to play the horses, a lifelong obsession that he first chronicled in his classic 1946 recording of "Race Track Blues."

Ignored by record producers and by most blues historians, Brown seemed resigned to his status. "I had some beautiful days," he reflected in 1984. "Now I have a little peace and quiet for myself, and I can enjoy the little things I wanna do. I have no regrets of nothing I have done. I had Cadillacs. I had five valets. I bought my grandfather things and helped my aunts build additions to their homes. When they weren't used to a hundred dollars, I'd give them twenty-five hundred dollars. I did it when they were here, but now they're dead and gone and in the grave and I don't have to cry no more. I put everybody in the graveyard happy. Listen, the world doesn't owe me nothin' 'cause I had it."

Brown's semiretirement was interrupted five years later when Bonnie Raitt asked him to tour as her opening act. With help from guitarist Danny Caron, Brown formed a combo of seasoned professionals capable of handling the complex chord progressions and subtle swing of his music and began recording for the Bullseye Blues label, then for Verve. Finally able to move beyond the blues mold that the music industry had cast him in more than half a century earlier, Brown now mixes Tin Pan Alley and Broadway standards and Liszt's *Hungarian Rhapsody No. 2 in C Minor* into his blues cocktail at festivals, concert halls, and jazz clubs throughout the world.

> At one point during the late 1940s, Charles Brown was one of the most famous jazz singers in the United States, epitomizing the Los Angeles nightclub artist—cool and nostalgic, defining the jazzman equivalent of film noir style.
> —Ben Sidran,
> **singer, pianist, writer, broadcaster, and record producer**

**Nat King Cole's trio with guitarist Oscar Moore was the model for brother Johnny Moore's Three Blazers, which featured Charles Brown. New York City, 1948**

LEFT:
**Brown influenced Fats Domino, who came from barrelhouse roots to become an icon of rock and roll. New Orleans, 1992**

ABOVE:
**Vocalist Ruth Brown was a huge Charles Brown booster during the 1980s, a period when it seemed as if most of the rest of the world had forgotten him. New York City, 1992**

LEFT:
**Brown said, "Back in the old days when honky tonk dives with piano players were popular, I would sneak to the back of the place and listen to the music of Ivory Joe Hunter and many others." London, 1961**

CHARLES BROWN

# Lightnin' Hopkins

The last of the pure country blues stylists to have a substantial commercial impact on African-American popular music during the early rhythm and blues era, Sam "Lightnin'" Hopkins (1912–1982) was a deeply soulful singer, a remarkable guitarist, and a poet of the first order. His specialty was spontaneous composition. Often making up lyrics as he went along, Hopkins committed hundreds of them to wax during his prolific recording career. The going rate was $100 a pop, cash on the spot. He didn't worry about royalties, because to Hopkins, it was the moment that counted most. As folklorist and record producer Mack McCormick once observed, "The true folksingers and their songs are birds in flight....[They] may be documented through manuscript and recording, but never captured."

Hopkins' songs reflected his experiences in the cotton fields and chain gangs of East Texas and the streets and bars of Houston's Third Ward. "You see," the long, lean bluesman explained to McCormick in 1960, "my songs are practically all *true* songs. They about something real to my way of knowing. Like all that has happened to me is liable to get into my songs. In my family they tell about my grandfather that was a slave that hung himself to escape bad treatment. Well, that's liable to be in one of my songs. Or that time I was out to Arizona—supposed to be pickin' cotton, but I got to gambling and then I got to going over to Mexico and bringing back wine and bootlegging it to them Indians on that government reservation. That's liable to be in a song. Or that time it was trouble up home, or when they got me on the county road gang, or had to say goodbye to some good girl, or be thinking of going to Galveston Beach—all that's liable to come up in my songs. Call 'em *true* songs."

Hopkins was born in Centerville, Texas, and raised in nearby Leona. His father was a musician, as were his five siblings. He made his first guitar out of a cigar box and chicken wire when he was eight years old, and shortly thereafter he picked up some pointers from and played along with the great Texas bluesman Blind Lemon Jefferson, a friend of the family. Hopkins hooked up with his cousin, vocalist and recording artist Alger "Texas" Alexander, during the late 1920s and spent several years roaming East Texas as his cousin's guitar accompanist. Alexander's sense of timing was highly irregular, not restricted to the standard twelve-bar blues form, and this also came to characterize Hopkins' music, thus making it difficult for other musicians to follow him. Many tried, but his best work was usually done alone.

After periods of living by his wits through gambling and other hustles and working with his wife as a sharecropper (an oppressive experience he immortalized in tunes like "Tim Moore's Farm," "I Asked the Bossman," and "Mr. Charlie"), he settled in Houston

> One night it's two police cars stop me and ask me where I got all my money. Say, "Where you been stealing?" I just show them this guitar and tell em, "This makes my living."
>
> —*Lightnin' Hopkins*

OPPOSITE:

**"[Lightnin' Hopkins] slept with his shades on," said record producer Bruce Bromberg. New York City, 1962**

**Chris Strachwitz (right) produced records by both Lightnin' Hopkins and fellow Texas bluesman Mance Lipscomb (left) for his Arhoolie record label. Monterey, California, 1973**

friends and neighbors in juke joints, on street corners, and while riding buses.

"He had no reason or desire to cater to the tastes of people who might come especially just to hear him and the songs that were making him famous via his records," producer Chris Strachwitz explained. "These songs were but a moment in his life, a thought or an observation."

As musical tastes among African-Americans changed, companies became less interested in recording Hopkins. By 1955, he was a forty-three-year-old has-been. In 1959, however, he was tracked down by folklorists Samuel Charters and Mack McCormick, who recorded him in earnest. He was no longer making singles for jukeboxes in black clubs and cafes, but rather entire albums of his musical musings for white folk-music fans. (The success of "Mojo Hand," a 1960 single for the New York–based Fire label, proved he still had viability in the African-American community, leading other labels to spin 45s off his LPs.)

Having found a new constituency among a college crowd weaned on the Kingston Trio, Hopkins overcame his reluctance to travel and followed the money. He became the toast of coffeehouses and folk festivals throughout the United States and Europe. He even overcame his fear of flying, documenting his first experience in the air in a 1961 blues titled "DC-7." A year later, after watching astronaut John Glenn orbit the earth on his landlady's television, Hopkins hurried to a Houston studio and cut a number he called "Happy Blues for John Glenn." The Texas bluesman had offered his personal reflections on a moment in time, collected his pay, and moved on to the next gig, leaving behind yet another poignant slice of sound and poetry for the world to savor.

around 1946 and was soon discovered by talent scout Lola Anne Cullen, who took him and pianist Wilson "Thunder" Smith to Los Angeles to record for the Aladdin label. The name "Lightnin'" was concocted for the occasion, and although the duo of Thunder and Lightnin' was short-lived, the moniker stuck.

Soon, Hopkins was recording not only for Aladdin, but for Gold Star and practically any other company willing to pay him in cash. Between 1949 and 1952, he scored five national R&B hits, including "Shotgun Blues" and "Give Me Central 209" (a.k.a. "Hello Central"), yet refused most offers to tour. He preferred to stick around Houston and entertain

ABOVE:
**Texas guitar slinger
Albert Collins was
influenced early
on by his cousin
Lightnin' Hopkins.
Chicago, 1987**

LEFT:
**Vocalist Barbara
Dane recorded an
album with Lightnin'
Hopkins in 1964.
Oakland, California,
1984**

# JOHN LEE HOOKER

The music of John Lee Hooker (b. 1917) has been described as atavistic, a throwback to the very origins of the blues before rules of rhyme, meter, and chord structure became standardized. It has also been called crude and primitive. As Pete Welding once argued, however, "It is perhaps more correct to consider it as music of extraordinary harmonic simplicity. He plays in the open guitar tunings usually associated with the older country blues, and his music is often modal. Interesting tensions are created by the superimposition of the standard blues harmonic patterns of his singing over the rhythmic, modal guitar patterns."

His skills honed in juke joints and at house-rent parties, Hooker hit in a big way when his first record, "Boogie Chillen," cut at a studio in the back of Bernie Bessman's Detroit record shop, topped *Billboard's* Most-Played Juke Box Race Records chart during the early months of 1949. Hooker's unaccompanied performance, delivered in a declarative baritone over an unchanging one-chord guitar pattern and the steady stomp of his foot on a wooden board, was not only a bold announcement of youthful independence—then and for generations to come—but marked the arrival of a wholly unique musical stylist. His roots were in an earlier time, yet through the use of heavily amplified guitar, Hooker was able to make them relevant to mass audiences both rural and urban. And while no one else sings and plays quite like him, his style has resonated throughout the music world ever since he waxed "Boogie Chillen." Evidence of his influence includes the 1950s recordings of Detroit sidekick Eddie Kirkland and Memphis-based bluesman Little Junior Parker; the

1960s rock of the Animals, the Rolling Stones, the Spencer Davis Group, Them (featuring Hooker vocal disciple Van Morrison), and Canned Heat; the work of ZZ Top and George Thorogood in the 1970s and 1980s; and in the 1990s the output of Hooker's daughter Zakiya, who launched her own recording career, and the Hooker-influenced Malian singer-guitarist Ali Farka Toure.

Hooker was born in Clarksdale, Mississippi. His father was a Baptist preacher who wouldn't allow him to bring his guitar into the house. His step-father, Will Moore, like Papa in "Boogie Chillen," encouraged the boy to boogie-woogie. Moore was a blues singer and guitarist himself, and Hooker credits him as his main influence. Although Moore was an associate of the great Charley Patton, he had grown up in Shreveport, Louisiana, a factor that made his style radically different from those of Patton and other Delta bluesmen. "It was basically hypnotic, one-chord drone blues, with darkly insistent vamping, violent treble-string punctuations, and songs that fitted both traditional and improvised lyrics into loose, chant-like structure," author and music historian Robert Palmer observed. Another early influence on Hooker was Tony Hollis, a Clarksdale-area singer-guitarist whose songs "Crawlin' King Snake" and "When My First Wife Left Me" became staples of the Hooker repertoire.

Hooker has not altered his own style over the years, though his musical surroundings have changed

> He's beloved worldwide as the king of the endless boogie, a genuine blues superstar whose droning, hypnotic one-chord grooves are at once both ultra-primitive and timeless.
> —Bill Dahl, writer

OPPOSITE:
"Since Muddy Waters' death, Hooker has become the grand old man of the blues." (Francis Davis, writer) Hooker, with saxophonist Ken Baker, at Yoshi's, Oakland, California, 1997

with the times. His earliest recordings were performed entirely solo. Attempts to wed his unorthodox bar and chord structures to a backing band produced often chaotic results at first. After he signed with the Chicago-based Vee-Jay label in 1955, however, his instrumental support grew more empathetic, thanks to the stellar work of such sidemen as guitarists Eddie Taylor and Lefty Bates.

By the early 1960s, Hooker had become one of the first postwar country bluesmen to be embraced by the so-called folk-blues movement, and he accommodated festival and coffeehouse crowds by performing alone, sometimes using acoustic guitar. Yet during the same period, he continued appealing to the R&B market with records that sported electric guitars, saxophones, and chirping background vocalists. The most successful of his R&B hits of that time was 1962's "Boom, Boom."

A hero to countless rock bands, Hooker began surrounding himself with young, rock-oriented players after moving from Detroit to the San Francisco Bay/Oakland area in 1970. *Endless Boogie*, the title of one of his albums from that period, quickly turned into a cliché. As poet and essayist Al Young noted, the Mississippi moaner's musicians "were playing nothing but what Hooker calls 'fast boogie' numbers all night long. A couple of times during the sets, Hooker would come forward and sit on a chair and play something solo, but mostly it was strictly rock and roll with a heavy blues backbeat."

For most of his prolific career, Hooker had recorded for nearly anyone willing to pay a cash advance, without regard for residuals. But the flow of new Hooker albums came to a grinding halt in 1977, when he decided that he'd been ripped off one time too many.

"It gets you to the place where you don't trust the record companies," he explained a few years later. "There's some good companies, but once you been burnt four or five times, you're scared of everybody. It's just like a wild dog: you wanna be good to him, but he's scared 'cause everybody he meets hits him, so when the good people come along that's not gonna hit him, he's scared of them too."

Hooker filed suits against several of his former labels, including Vee-Jay, as well as one against the major retail chain Tower Records, an unusual action since manufacturers, not retailers, are responsible for royalty payments. The bluesman's attorney argued, however, that record stores are part of the "chain of aiding and abetting a copyright infringement"—that they are the "tail of the dog," so to speak. Hooker eventually reached out-of-court settlements with Vee-Jay and Tower.

With his business affairs finally in order, Hooker turned to a former sideman, guitarist Roy Rogers, to produce *The Healer*, his first new recording in a dozen years. The lovingly crafted 1989 disc featured guest appearances by, among others, Carlos Santana, Robert Cray, George Thorogood, Los Lobos, and Bonnie Raitt, whose duet with Hooker on "I'm in the Mood" netted both singers a Grammy for Best Traditional Blues Recording. Rogers continued working with Hooker on subsequent albums, teaming the venerable bluesman with such heavyweights as Charles Brown, Albert Collins, Ry Cooder, Booker T. Jones, Keith Richards, and Van Morrison (who later produced Hooker). Rogers also let Hooker go solo, as he had in the beginning, his brooding baritone voice, sparse yet rhythmically propulsive guitar strokes, and pounding foot creating mesmerizing blues and boogies of timeless quality.

ABOVE:

**Hooker has been a hero to many rock players, including the Animals. Copenhagen, 1966**

ABOVE:

**ZZ Top, another rock band strongly influenced by John Lee Hooker. Memphis, Tennessee, 1981**

ABOVE:

**John Lee's daughter, Zakiya Hooker, has her own singing career and often opens for her father. Oakland, California, 1997**

JOHN LEE HOOKER

# MUDDY WATERS

McKINLEY MORGANFIELD (1915–1983) DIDN'T KNOW QUITE what to expect when he made his first trip overseas. On the recommendation of his old pal Big Bill Broonzy (a star of pre–World War II city blues who'd been wowing Europeans since 1951 with his retro-country-blues routines), the Mississippi-born, Chicago-based bluesman popularly known as Muddy Waters hooked up a modest British tour in 1958. There weren't enough funds for him to bring his whole band, but he did manage to persuade the promoters to let pianist Otis Spann, who understood Waters' music better than anyone, come along. Traditional jazz trombonist Chris Barber's band was recruited to provide the accompaniment.

The opening night audience, which had been primed on New Orleans-style jazz and skiffle music, as well as on pseudo-country blues of the Broonzy and Josh White varieties, was horrified at what it heard, especially by Waters' screaming slide guitar. "When Muddy Waters came to England," writer Paul Oliver commented in *Jazz Monthly*, "his rocking blues and electric guitar [were] meat that proved too strong for many stomachs."

Barber urged Waters to turn his amp down, which he did the following evening, much to most everyone's relief. "Now I know that the people in England like soft guitar and the old blues," Waters told *Melody Maker* before returning home to Chicago. "Next time I come I'll learn some old songs first."

> Muddy's band became a sort of blues graduate school in much the same way that Art Blakey's Jazz Messengers and the Miles Davis groups were in jazz during the same era.
> —Francis Davis, writer

Waters, of course, knew plenty of old songs. "Walkin' Blues," recorded by Waters for Chess Records in 1950, was a Robert Johnson tune, which in turn had been inspired by Son House's "My Black Mama." (Johnson and House were two of Waters' main musical heroes.) "Louisiana Blues," the record that in 1951 established Waters as a major attraction among African-Americans in the United States, was an adaptation of the Delta blues standard "Rollin' 'n' Tumblin'." There were others, too, but Waters rendered all of them in a way that at the time seemed sacrilegious to listeners with moldy-fig (staunch jazz traditionalist) and folklorist notions about what blues should and shouldn't be.

Although Waters was but one of thousands of blues guitar players who switched from acoustic to electric during the rural-to-urban migration of the World War II period, he didn't simply play amplified guitar in front to a scaled-down jazz orchestra, as did many of his contemporaries. Muddy Waters invented the electric blues ensemble. Many of his early Aristocrat and Chess recordings featured him with only bass accompaniment, but in Chicago juke joints during the late 1940s—with Little Walter blowing distorted harmonica through a beat-up amp, Jimmy Rogers adding rhythmically propulsive lines on a second electric guitar, and drummer Baby Face Leroy Foster kicking a heavy backbeat—Waters devised a revolutionary new style of the blues.

**OPPOSITE:**
**Writer Bill Dahl said of Muddy Waters, "From the late 1940s on, he eloquently defined [Chicago's] aggressive, swaggering, Delta-rooted sound with his declamatory vocals and piercing slide guitar attack." Boston, 1966**

He updated the Mississippi Delta blues of his plantation upbringing for the second half of the twentieth century, prefiguring the music that eventually became known as rock and roll.

Leonard Chess was slow in realizing the commercial potential of Waters' new electric ensemble style and continued to produce sessions that featured Waters (himself electrified) and acoustic bassist Big Crawford in a rather traditional Delta vein. Chess began giving in, albeit gradually, at first adding Little Walter the 1950 session that yielded "Louisiana Blues" and 1951's "Long Distance Call." At the end of 1951, though, Chess brought the whole band—Waters, Walter, Rogers, and new drummer Elgin Evans—into the studio for the first time. Spann joined in 1953 and helped to provide the backbone for Waters' most successful period on the R&B charts—from 1954 to 1955—when he scored four top five hits in a row:

"I'm Your Hoochie Coochie Man," "Just Make Love to Me," "I'm Ready," and "Manish Boy." With the addition around 1956 of bassist Andrew Stephenson, the instrumentation of the classic Muddy Waters blues ensemble was complete.

A triumphant appearance at the 1960 Newport Jazz Festival, where the excitement rose to incendiary levels during "Got My Mojo Workin'," marked the beginning of Waters' breakthrough into white America. Just the same, it took the endorsements a few years down the line of such open-minded Brits as the Rolling Stones (who lifted their name from a 1950 Waters recording) and the Beatles to make it possible for the bluesman to land the type of lucrative concert bookings that eventually made him a relatively wealthy man.

Waters was a generous man. Not only did he give his blessings to the solo careers of such sidemen as Little Walter, Junior Wells, and James Cotton, but he frequently invited young, unknown players to sit in with the band. Paul Butterfield and Michael Bloomfield were among the many beneficiaries of Waters' bandstand benevolence.

By the 1970s, Waters was firmly established as an international attraction. His band no longer boasted sidemen of such stellar note—Otis Spann, who died in 1970 a year after leaving the band, had been the last of them—but it was a solid ensemble that followed with aplomb the musical formulas Waters had devised years earlier. (Waters, whose sense of timing was unique, was not an easy musician to follow.) The sting of his slide guitar and the declamatory nature of his vocals retained their authority, the mark of a self-made man who had taken Delta blues to the city, refashioned it to fit his unique vision, played as loud as he pleased, and changed the course of popular music in the process.

MUDDY WATERS

**Michael Bloomfield frequently sat in with Muddy's band. Chicago, 1960**

OPPOSITE:
**Jimmy Rogers recalled, "Muddy's cousin was telling him I was a nice person.... He kinda trusted me to talk to and be with, so we got to be really good friends. Then we started rehearsing and playing together and building that big mountain that we built." Oakland, California, 1997**

ABOVE:
**James Cotton, one of the fine harp players that followed the remarkable Little Walter into the Waters band. Cambridge, Massachusetts, 1964**

# Howlin' Wolf

A LARGE, INTIMIDATING MAN WHO STOOD SIX FEET THREE INCHES (191cm) and weighed close to three hundred pounds (136kg), Chester Burnett (1910–1976) was known by a number of names during his storied life. Some called him "Bull Cow," others "Big Foot Chester," but the one that stuck, allegedly given to him by his grandfather when Chester was a boy of three, was "Howlin' Wolf." Although the nickname referred to the four-legged beasts that roamed the woods in Monroe County, Mississippi, the old man had unknowingly foretold the coming of one of the most fearsome voices in the annals of American vernacular music.

"He had a voice like shattered glass being dragged over hot asphalt," commented critic Mark Humphrey. "It enabled him to register rage, paranoia, loneliness, and lust almost as a single emotion clenched into a taut vocal fist that punched like none other on earth."

Born in West Point, Mississippi, Wolf moved with his family to the Delta, near Ruleville, in 1923 and eventually came under the tutelage of two Mississippi Delta blues masters. Charley Patton, who entertained farm laborers around Will Dockery's plantation (a place that seems to have spawned more than its share of bluesmen), gave the young Wolf pointers on the guitar Wolf's father had bought for him in 1928. Patton's harsh growl also left its mark, as did his extroverted performing style. "When he played his guitar," Wolf later told Pete Welding, "he would turn it over backwards and forwards and throw it around on his shoulders, between his legs, throw it up in the sky." Patton also contributed to Wolf's repertoire; years later, reworkings of such Patton themes as "Hook Up My Pony and Saddle Up My Old Black Mare," "Spoonful," and "Banty Rooster" turned up in the Howlin' Wolf songbook. And briefly married to Wolf's half-sister was Aleck "Rice" Miller, the harmonica virtuoso who became famous in the 1950s after he adopted the name of deceased Chicago blues star Sonny Boy Williamson.

Armed with an acoustic guitar and a harmonica mounted on a rack, Wolf entertained on weekends throughout the 1930s, sometimes playing with such musicians as Robert Johnson, Robert Jr. Lockwood, and Willie Brown, but his weekdays were spent as a cotton farmer. Even after a four-year stint spent mostly near Seattle in the Signal Corps during World War II, he returned to the land for his living. In 1948, while farming in West Memphis, Arkansas, Wolf decided to get serious about his musical career. He landed a daily fifteen-minute slot on the radio station KWEM and sold advertising time to a local seed company. Most importantly, he formed a band that played between the farm reports, which he delivered himself.

The combo, billed as the House Rockers, was as raw and raucous as they come. Willie Steele pounded the traps unmercifully, a piano player known as "Destruction" banged the 88s, and Willie Johnson picked an electric guitar cranked up so as to produce

> They call my kind of music folk songs. But them no folk songs. Them old blues.
> —Howlin' Wolf

OPPOSITE:
**"Howlin' Wolf had a voice like shattered glass being dragged over hot asphalt," wrote Mark Humphry. "It enabled him to register rage, paranoia, loneliness, and lust almost as a single emotion clenched into a taut vocal fist that punched like none other on earth." Cambridge, Massachussetts, 1966**

a torturous distortion that, in the words of historian Cub Koda, "aurally extended and amplified the violence and nastiness" of the music. And cutting through the din with otherworldly authority was the Wolf's ferocious howl and hard-riffing harmonica.

**"It was only fitting that when the Rolling Stones made their American TV debut on <u>Shindig</u> in 1964, they stipulated that the Wolf also be featured on the broadcast." (Francis Davis, writer)**
**New York City, 1980**

In 1951, Wolf caught the ears of up-and-coming Memphis record producer Sam Phillips and made his first recordings. The initial release, which appeared on Chess Records in Chicago, was the haunting one-chord "Moaning at Midnight," backed with the more conventional "How Many More Years." ("Wolf sings the standard blues I-IV-V changes," Humphrey said of the latter, "but his House Rockers, as if mesmerized by their own groove, never leave the I chord.") Both sides registered on *Billboard*'s R&B top ten. At age forty-one, Howlin' Wolf was a blues star.

Recording concurrently for Chess and the Los Angeles–based RPM label for a period, sometimes cutting the same songs for each, Wolf moved to Chicago around 1953 and cast his lot with Chess, with which he remained for the rest of his career. Willie Johnson joined him for a while, but Hubert Sumlin eventually took over the lead guitar slot in the band and became Wolf's most empathetic musical foil.

Most of Wolf's songs were original compositions or his adaptations of Delta standards, but between 1960 and 1963 bassist-producer Willie Dixon supplied much of the material. Wolf complained bitterly about having his arm twisted into recording such Dixon tunes as "Wang Dang Doodle," "Backdoor Man," "The Red Rooster," and "I Ain't Superstitious." The composer sometimes had to threaten to give them to Muddy Waters, Wolf's archrival at Chess, before the cantankerous singer would agree to do them, but they turned out to be among the most enduring numbers in his repertoire.

Wolf's performances were as intense as his singing. He would sometimes make his entrance at clubs by crawling on all fours through the audience to the stage, snapping and hissing at customers as he moved. When playing guitar, he was known to roll and wiggle on the floor and even do somersaults.

Although his string of hit records had ended by the mid-1960s, Wolf became the idol of a generation of rock musicians. The Rolling Stones, who had recorded a version of "The Red Rooster," stipulated that ABC-TV book him as their guest on *Shindig* in 1965; the British band sat worshipfully at his feet while their hero delivered "How Many More Years" for his network television debut. Other rock artists, including the Doors, Cream, and Led Zeppelin, also recorded Wolf's songs.

Bassist-composer
Willie Dixon's blues
songs were an impor-
tant part of Wolf's
repertoire.
Chicago, 1968

HOWLIN' WOLF

RIGHT:

**"Wolf never amounted to much of an instrumentalist," Francis Davis wrote. "Once settled in Chicago, he wisely assigned most of the guitar work to the fiery Hubert Sumlin."**

**Chicago, 1988**

# LITTLE WALTER

HARMONICA VIRTUOSO MARION WALTER JACOBS (1930–1968) jumped when he first heard the sound of his own success blasting out of a radio in Shreveport, Louisiana, during the late summer of 1952. Little Walter, as he was known professionally, was on tour with the Muddy Waters band, and the sound he heard was an instrumental shuffle he'd recorded several months earlier at the end of one of Waters' sessions for Chess Records in Chicago. Originally titled "Your Cat Will Play," it had been serving as a number that Waters' sidemen played at gigs before their boss hit the stage. The company had retitled the tune "Juke" and issued it under Walter's name on its Checker subsidiary. Taken by surprise at hearing it on the air, Walter quit the band on the spot, returned to Chicago, took over fellow harp blower Junior Wells' band, the Aces (Wells himself took Walter's place in Waters' band), renamed them the Night Cats (later the Jukes), and hit the road to cash in on the record's success.

Little Walter, born in Marksville, Louisiana, never looked back. Although the Chicago-based musician did, at Leonard Chess' insistence, continue recording as a Waters sideman for several more years, he was now on his own and flying. "Juke" became a bona fide smash—the best-selling platter to date for Chess/Checker—rising to the top of *Billboard*'s Best Selling Retail Rhythm & Blues Records chart, where it

> His daring instrumental innovations were so fresh, startling, and ahead of their time that they sometimes sported a jazz sensibility, soaring and swooping in front of snarling guitars and swinging rhythms perfectly suited to Walter's pioneering flights of fancy.
> —*Bill Dahl,* writer

rested for a week, and to the peak of the Most-Played Juke Box Rhythm & Blues Records chart, where it reigned for eight weeks. Over the next seven years, Walter placed thirteen more songs on *Billboard*'s various R&B top ten lists, with 1955's "My Babe," a vocal number that bassist-producer Willie Dixon had adapted for Walter from the spiritual "This Train," becoming the biggest of all. During the 1950s his success eclipsed that of Waters and of Chess' other major blues star, Howlin' Wolf. In fact, Walter appeared at the Apollo and other leading African-American theaters, sharing the bill with such artists as B.B. King and Ray Charles, while Waters and Wolf were still playing clubs.

Although Walter had been blowing harmonica through a cheap microphone plugged into a guitar amplifier during his post–World War II days as a busker along Chicago's Maxwell Street (where shopkeepers rented musicians access to electric outlets), this powerful new sound wasn't captured on wax until Walter's 1951 recordings with Waters of "Country Boy" and "She Moves Me." The sound became a trademark of Walter's subsequent recordings, both with Muddy Waters and on his own, and profoundly influenced the music of virtually every other blues harp blower who came after him. "The legacy of Marion 'Little Walter' Jacobs is a musical mirror so brilliant and expansive that today it is impossible to find a blues harp player who is not seen most clearly when reflected in it," wrote harmonica authority Kim Field.

OPPOSITE:

**"[Little Walter Jacobs] is probably the single most innovative performer in the history of the blues." (Peter Guralnick, writer) London, 1964**

**Guitarist Robert Jr. Lockwood—stepson of the legendary Robert Johnson, who taught him to play—recorded with Little Walter in the 1950s. Paris, 1982**

RIGHT:
**Big Walter Horton had a big influence on Little Walter the young. Copenhagen, 1968**

Greatly influenced by Big Walter "Shakey" Horton and Aleck "Rice" Miller (also known as "Sonny Boy Williamson"), both of whom had coached Little Walter when he was a teenager, Walter had also listened intently to the searing alto saxophone of proto-R&B superstar Louis Jordan and to riff-based numbers by the Count Basie big band. From these influences, Walter fashioned a revolutionary, jazz-imbued blues harp style that was simultaneously graceful and gritty, alternately fierce and tender.

"His sense of dynamics and tonal variety gave him an unrivaled flowing inventiveness, swooping and driving on rockers and dance boogies, or soft and melancholy on slow numbers," author Giles Oakley once observed. "The harp would seem to be drifting away, when suddenly he would crash back up front with fierce stabbing notes only to turn back to a floating dreaminess. His quiet and sad voice made him John Lee Hooker's favorite singer, but he is best remembered for his eerily mournful harp, which has remained unsurpassedly influential in popular music as a whole."

Sadly, Walter's string of hits came to a screeching halt at the end of the 1950s. He did not adapt well to this change of fortune, and the unruliness that had been a hallmark of his youth—he'd run away from home at age twelve and spent the bulk of his teen years playing for spare change on street corners and in clubs—quickly returned to the fore.

Walter continued performing, even touring Europe and England (where, in 1964, the Rolling Stones served as his backup band) and recording on

> Walter's swooping, sliding, charging harp work was a crucial part of the roof-shaking sound that was developed to cut through the noise of South Side clubs.
> —Chris Norris, writer

LITTLE WALTER

occasion during the 1960s, but his singing took on a pronounced alcoholic slur and his harp blowing became unfocused, greatly weakened by a collapsed lung. He missed more than a few engagements, and when he did bother to show up, he'd blame his sidemen for his erratic performances and sometimes wave a loaded pistol onstage. He had no permanent residence during his last few years other than Muddy Waters' basement, where his old employer would allow him to crash.

Famous for his quick temper, Walter needed little provocation to make him combative. A badly scarred countenance made him appear to be a much older man than he actually was. He suffered the worst in a February 1968 street brawl, during which he sustained a blood clot that led to his death from coronary thrombosis. When he died, Little Walter was not yet thirty-eight years old.

**Aleck "Rice" Miller, known professionally as Sonny Boy Williamson, a witty and driving harpist and singer, coached the teenaged Little Walter. Paris, 1964**

# B.B. KING

**OPPOSITE:**

**"The true measure of his success is that B.B. King's music...has shaped and colored modern blues to such a degree that virtually no performer of the music since his time has escaped the pull of its pervasive influence." (Pete Welding, writer) Boston, 1967**

**RIGHT:**

**"Guitarist Charlie Christian's only match for lyricism, harmonic invention and earthiness was Lester Young, [the star tenor sax] soloist in [Count] Basie's band." Both Christian and Young (shown here at the 1958 Newport Jazz Festival) were heroes to King. (Francis Davis, writer) Newport, Rhode Island, 1958**

"B.B. KING IS THE ONLY STRAIGHT BLUES SINGER IN AMERICA with a large, adult, nationwide, and almost entirely Negro audience," Charles Keil wrote in the book *Urban Blues*. "If the adjectives 'unique,' 'pure,' and 'authentic' apply to any blues singer alive today, they certainly apply to B.B. King."

It has now been more than three decades since the sociologist made that observation in his groundbreaking book, which featured B.B. King (b. 1925)—wailing with mouth open wide, one hand grasping a microphone and the other to his ear in order to better maintain pitch over his band's riffing horn section—on the cover. *Urban Blues* was the first work to state the thesis that blues singers like King serve as the secular counterpart of the preacher in the African-American community, that the interaction between the blues-

> Maybe our forefathers couldn't keep their language together when they were taken away from Africa, but this—the blues—was a language we invented to let people know we had something to say. And we've been saying it pretty strong ever since.
> —B.B. King

man and his audience during a performance is very much like that between preacher and congregation during worship.

It's been almost forty years since King recorded *Live at the Regal*, the album that best demonstrates Keil's argument. The proof is in the grooves: members of the black Chicago audience respond to King's every vocal and guitar line, sometimes individually, more often en masse, with shouts of concurrence and screams of approval. His every concern, trial, hurt, joy, and longing become theirs. Through affirmation, the pain of everyday life is lifted off the audience's shoulders—if only temporarily, in a kind of catharsis—and at the same time, the joys of day-to-day human interaction are gloriously exalted.

"Those who suspect that the driving force behind the blues will disappear in the harmonious and fully integrated society that Reverend Martin Luther King envisions are probably mistaken," Keil speculated, "because it is conflict between the sexes more than conflict between cultures that motivates the blues artist to bring his troubles before a sympathetic audience."

What Keil didn't foresee, besides the fact that Dr. King's dream would be far from realized more than three decades later, is that "pure" blues (not just permutations thereof as represented by rock and rollers like Elvis Presley, Chuck Berry, and the Rolling Stones) would find large white acceptance within a few years of his writing. Hailed for their innovations and credited with immense influence by such guitar gods of the late-1960s rock culture as Eric Clapton and Michael Bloomfield, King and other bluesmen suddenly found themselves playing before predominately white audiences. Simultaneously, their following among African-Americans began to decline.

Today, B.B. King is an icon of U.S. culture, acknowledged by blacks and whites alike as the king of the blues—and rightly so. No other blues artist has had a wider influence, instrumentally and vocally. His electric guitar innovations—sustained cries achieved through the combined use of finger trills, the bending of strings, and controlled feedback—set the standard for both blues and rock players, and his picking prowess remains quite formidable. And while wear and tear on

the larynx have diminished his ability to hit those chilling falsetto wails that were his trademark in the 1950s, King remains a highly commanding vocalist.

Born Riley B. King in Indianola, Mississippi, he grew up amid poverty, domestic turmoil, and tragedy. His parents, both farmhands, separated when he was four years old. He then lived with his mother, who died when he was nine, and next with his grandmother, who died the following year.

King began singing early on and, at age twelve, while living with an aunt and uncle, started experimenting with a guitar that a visiting preacher brought to their house. Unlike many blues artists who were influenced primarily by the music of their immediate surroundings, King had bigger ears (so to speak).

King was, of course, affected by the raw Mississippi Delta blues of his famous cousin, Bukka White. Yet on his aunt's Victrola he heard music from other regions, particularly the anguished Texas country blues of Blind Lemon Jefferson and the decidedly urbane single-string guitar work of Lonnie Johnson, who recorded prolifically in New York and Chicago

both on his own and in the company of such jazz giants as Louis Armstrong and Duke Ellington.

The ascendency of the electric guitar in the early 1940s—by Charlie Christian with Benny Goodman, then by Texas bluesman T-Bone Walker—had a profound impact on King's developing style. Other important guitar influences ranged from the sophisticated stylings of European jazzman Django Reinhardt and brothers Oscar Moore (of the King Cole Trio) and Johnny Moore (of the Three Blazers, featuring Charles Brown) to the down-home, Robert Johnson–inspired slide work of Elmore James. King also listened closely to the jump blues of Louis Jordan and the Tympany Five and to the big band jazz of Count Basie, paying special attention to the manner in which horn riffs were fashioned around Jimmy Rushing's vocals and to the liquid phrasing and bent notes of tenor saxophonist Lester Young. By combining these influences—the high with the low, if you will—he crafted, through trial and error, the distinctive B.B. King guitar approach.

King's vocal influences are a bit harder to pinpoint. Some historians, including Charlie Gillett and Peter Guralnick, have cited New Orleans rhythm and blues shouter Roy Brown as the source of King's wailing style, though King himself disputes this. Instead, he credits Chicago-based bluesman Doctor Clayton, Nashville gospel singer Sam McCrary (of the Fairfield Four), and Blind Lemon Jefferson. "Those three guys in about equal parts shaped my style," King told Charles Keil in 1963, "but I don't think I ever sounded like any one of them—more of a mixture plus my own contribution."

Although largely self-taught, King did take a few lessons from Robert Johnson's stepson, Robert Jr. Lockwood, who attempted to show King how to play rhythm guitar. King never did master the art of accompanying his own singing. Instead, he developed a call-and-response pattern of alternating his powerful vocal lines with dazzling single-string obligatos, thus setting the stage for urban blues as we know it today.

"If it were not for B.B. King," Michael Bloomfield stated in 1979, "there would be no [Eric] Clapton, no [George] Harrison, no [Jeff] Beck. There'd be no lead guitar, no rock and roll as we know it."

**B. B. King at the Newport Folk Festival of 1968, which also featured Buddy Guy, Junior Wells, and Janis Joplin with Big Brother and the Holding Company. Newport, Rhode Island, 1968**

B.B. KING

OPPOSITE:
**Buddy Guy has said, "B.B. King is the only person who has ever shown me anything on the guitar. Other than what he taught me, I'm completely self-taught." Cambridge, Massachusetts, 1963**

LEFT:
**B.B. King's stylistic disciple Otis Rush said, "If it's got soul or some kind of feelings, I love it, but my thing is the blues. Blues come from the hard work slavery times when you worked from sun-up to sundown, and when you can't have anything but the blues." New York City, 1987**

# Bobby Bland

Little has changed for Bobby Bland (b. 1930) since he scored his first major hit, "Farther Up the Road," in 1957. Despite attempts by ABC Records during the mid-1970s to establish him in the pop market (as the company had done a few years before with his early Memphis cohort, B.B. King), Bland remains largely unknown outside the African-American community. The blues and soul singer still performs mostly one-nighters on the so-called chitlin circuit, traveling by bus with his band sometimes as far as six hundred miles (965km) between engagements.

The ritual surrounding Bland's performances hasn't changed much, either. A massive man with a broad nose and high cheekbones, Bland strolls casually to the stage in a well-tailored suit, grabs the microphone in a tight fist, and begins purring in a smooth, slightly nasal baritone. Then he throws his head back and lets loose a roar, with brassy horn blasts and drum punches adding emphasis. Key phrases begin with tortured vowel sounds broken into wailing melismas.

As he sings, Bland concentrates on his own voice and on his nine-piece orchestra, which still plays many of onetime bandleader Joe Scott's arrangements of tunes like "I'll Take Care of You," "Don't Cry No More," "That's the Way Love Is," "Ain't Nothing You Can Do," and "Call It Stormy Monday" that have been in the book since the 1960s. The vocalist's eyes focus on the ceiling through much of his performance, yet he gives the illusion that he's singing personally to every listener in the room, evidence of an incredibly charismatic performance style that seems to affect his female fans in particular.

At every familiar turn of phrase, women scream answers and wave their hands high. "Sing it, Bobby!" "Well, all right!" Some shout out lyrics, anticipating what Bland will sing a bar or two later. The dynamic is much like that of a religious congregation, where the preacher's personal magnetism sometimes provides a greater stimulus than the literal message he's delivering. The din is sometimes so great that it is difficult to hear the singer clearly.

Women dressed to the nines approach the stage one or two at a time, stand in front of Bland, and take turns having Polaroids snapped. Sometimes Bland's bodyguard, a tall, muscular man with a shaved head, stops them. Other times he allows them to indulge themselves. Bland remains largely unfazed by the sideshow in front of him, though he occasionally pauses to kid or sometimes kiss an admirer.

When Bland sings the line "You told me to hit the road" in "The Feeling Is Gone," the six horn players exit the stage for about ten minutes while the guitar player takes a long, slow blues ride in the manner of T-Bone Walker. "Take your time, son; take your time," Bland commands gently.

Bland is one of the few major blues stars who doesn't play a guitar or other musical instrument, which may explain why few white blues fans have

> As shamlessly emotive and wondrously expressive as any gospel singer (he did, in fact, emerge from a church background), Bland is especially popular with women. No wonder. His songs are addressed directly to them.
> —Francis Davis,
> **writer**

**OPPOSITE:**
**"Bland isn't one of your warm ethnic types. He doesn't even play guitar. He's a romantic, like Jimmy Witherspoon, cutting the sweat and grease with a little moonlight and roses." (Michele Lomax, writer) Emeryville, California, 1997**

taken to his music. He once thought about taking up the guitar, but that would have required that he cut his nails, which he keeps long, immaculately manicured, and handsomely polished.

Robert Calvin Bland was born in Rosemark, Tennessee, about thirty miles (48km) from Memphis. His first love was the music of gospel quartets like the Five Blind Boys of Mississippi and the Dixie Hummingbirds. (The influence of Ira Tucker, the Hummingbirds' lead singer, showed up later in Bland's blues style.) In 1950, he hooked up with the Beale Streeters, a confederation of Memphis bluesmen under B.B. King's leadership that also included vocalist Rosco Gordon and pianist Johnny Ace. Bland and Gordon served as warm-up acts for their leader, with Bland doubling as King's chauffeur.

After making a few unsuccessful sides for Chess and Modern in 1951 and 1952, Bland signed with the fledgling Memphis-based Duke label later in 1952 and landed an opening slot on fast-rising labelmate Ace's touring show. In 1953, while Bland was stationed in Japan with the U.S. Army, Houston promoter Don Robey gained control of Duke and continued a chain of contractual obligations involving Bland that would last until 1985. (During that time, Duke was sold to ABC in 1973 and ABC to MCA in 1979.) "It was kind of a lifetime thing that I had signed, not really knowing what I was doing and having no advisement or anything," the vocalist stated in 1983.

Upon his discharge from the Army in 1955, he began recording for Robey in Houston and was placed under the creative guidance of trumpeter-arranger Joe Scott, who helped shape Bland's style over the next few years. His approach became less imitative of B.B. King's, and his declarative midrange was punctuated by piercing falsetto screams and deep, throaty squalls. Bland toured the country incessantly as part

of Blues Consolidated—a package show headlined by fellow Duke artist Little Junior Parker and featuring Scott's orchestra—from 1955 until 1962, by which time Bland's popularity had eclipsed Parker's. Bland took Scott's jazz-imbued band with him when he left Parker.

In 1985, Bland finally broke his contractual chains with MCA and signed with Malaco. The Jackson, Mississippi company, which has cornered the soul-blues market with a roster that now also includes Johnnie Taylor, Little Milton, Denise LaSalle, and Tyrone Davis, produces thoughtfully crafted if predictable albums by Bland aimed at the now middle-aged working-class African-American audience that has always been his fan base. The high and low ends of his voice have been chiseled away by the wear and tear of four decades worth of one-nighters, but "the lion of the blues," as critic Michele Lomax dubbed Bland, keeps on crooning the blues and soul ballads in a distinctive baritone that retains much of its original warmth and power.

RIGHT: **Ike Turner (seen here with Tina Turner) played piano on a 1952 Bobby Bland record date in Memphis. Copenhagen, Denmark, 1972**

BOBBY BLAND

From 1955 to 1962
Bland toured in a
blues show headlined
by Little Junior
Parker. As his
popularity grew, he
struck out on his own,
taking the show's
band with him.
Chicago, 1963

LEFT:
Bobby Bland
recalled, "Wayne
Bennett worked
eight years with me
on the road....We got
together on a lot of
things, like ideas, dif-
ferent phrases, and
how to approach a
note, and I must say
that he taught me
quite a bit, because
it kinda grew me
into a blues ballad
thing."
Chicago, 1986

BOBBY BLAND

# ALBERT KING

WHILE THERE IS NO DENYING THE IMMEASURAB... modern blues and rock musicians... Walker, the first bluesman to... amplifier, and to B.B. Kin... back and more to W... (1923–1992) was... tar stylist from... disciple, early in his... even claimed to be B.B.... (Both men *were* born in Indianola, Mississippi.) But by the time Albert signed with Stax Records in 1966, he had developed a highly personal guitar style marked by economical, rhythmically propulsive single-note lines and a tone produced by picking with his left thumb while bending wildly with his right fingers on the strings of a right-handed Flying V guitar turned upside down and tuned to an open E minor chord. His groundbreaking, soul-imbued recordings for the Memphis firm from 1966 to 1973 defined the state of modern blues during that period, and had a vast and lasting impact on guitar players on both sides of the Atlantic. Not only did King's unique style alter the approaches of such already established blues guitarists as Otis Rush and Albert Collins, but it had a tremendous influence on younger musicians like Eric Clapton, Jimmy Page, Jimi Hendrix, and Stevie Ray Vaughan.

One of thirteen children, King was raised by his mother in Forrest City, Arkansas. As a youth, he

...made... him." ..."...itar" consisted ...ed to the wall of ...hat he picked with a ...Later, he bought an ...oustic guitar for $1.25, and eventually graduated to an electric model purchased for $125 at a pawnshop in Little Rock. After practicing for a few years, he began sitting in around Osceola, Arkansas, with a group called Yancey's Band. "They learned me my chords and what key was what," the six-foot-four-inch (193cm) blues titan explained. "I didn't know but two or three songs. The trumpet player stayed on my case all the time. I wanted to use a clamp on my neck, but he made me throw that clamp away and I had to make the chords with my hand."

Driving a bulldozer during the day, King formed his own group, the In the Groove Boys. "I learned 'em those three songs that I knew," he remembered with a chuckle, "and we'd play 'em fast, slow, and medium, but we got over."

After singing with the Harmony Kings gospel quartet in South Bend, Indiana, and playing drums for

his... on a... —Alb... writer

*[inset card: BUSINESS REPLY MAIL — FIRST-CLASS MAIL PERMIT NO. 1158 BOULDER, CO — POSTAGE WILL BE PAID BY ADDRESSEE — HOT ROD MAGAZINE — PO BOX 51397 — BOULDER CO 80323-1397 — NO POSTAGE NECESSARY IF MAILED IN THE UNITED STATES — SEE OTHER SIDE FOR SPECIAL SAVINGS! — Printed on Recycled Paper]*

**OPPOSITE:**
**Albert King had a powerful effect on the playing of the young British rockers Eric Clapton and Jimmy Page. Chicago, 1987**

**Eric Clapton first began borrowing King's licks and solos when he played with the trio Cream. Boston, 1967**

The crisp Stax sound, which had propelled such soul singers as Carla and Rufus Thomas, William Bell, Otis Redding, Wilson Pickett, and Eddie Floyd onto the charts, was now being applied to the blues and proved an immediate success.

King's seminal Stax 45s, which also included "Crosscut Saw" and "Born Under a Bad Sign," were initially bought primarily by African-American consumers. With the introduction of "underground" FM radio in 1967, however, King's razor-edged sound began to cross over, and white listeners—who'd already been primed by Eric Clapton's incorporation of King licks and solos into his popular sides with the power-rock trio Cream—were drawn to King's soulful blues in large numbers. His 1968 debut at San Francisco's Fillmore Auditorium (rock impresario Bill Graham had gone all the way to East St. Louis to offer King $1,600 to play three nights at the Fillmore on a bill with Jimi Hendrix and John Mayall and the Blues Breakers) solidified King's crossover following, and he remained until his death one of the few blues artists to consistently attract substantial numbers of both black and white fans.

As Michael Bloomfield pointed out in 1977 to Dan Forte of *Guitar Player*: "Between Al Jackson's productions, the Booker T. and the MGs rhythm section, the choice of material, the Memphis Horns, and Albert's playing, he was the only bluesman I know of who had a completely comfortable synthesis with modern black music—R&B, so to speak—and sold copiously to a black audience as well as to the white audience. He was the only singer who had clever, modern arrangements that would fit in with the black radio market *and* with the white market and in no way compromised his style. That's sort of amazing, in that B.B. King never did it, except once with 'The Thrill Is Gone,' but Albert did it time after time."

Jimmy Reed in Gary, King made his first record, "Bad Luck Blues," for the Parrot label in Chicago in 1953. The title proved prophetic, however, and he returned to Osceola for a while, then settled in East St. Louis, Illinois, where he began recording for Bobbin in 1959. He scored his first national hit, "Don't Throw Your Love on Me So Strong," two years later on the King label out of Cincinnati.

King didn't return to the charts until 1966, when his recording of "Laundromat Blues" for Stax became one of that year's biggest blues hits. The innovative melding of King's dry, husky baritone voice and bent-note guitar with the exacting drive of the Stax house rhythm section (rhythm guitarist Steve Cropper, keyboardists Booker T. Jones and Isaac Hayes, bassist Donald "Duck" Dunn, and drummer Al Jackson, Jr.) and the Mar-Keys' punching horn section (later known as the Memphis Horns) brought blues into the soul era.

ABOVE:
**British bluesman John Mayall (left) produced one of Albert King's later Stax albums. Guitarist Donald Kinsey (right) worked with King before joining reggae superstar Bob Marley's band. Merrilville, Indiana, 1988**

RIGHT:
**Three-fourths of the famous Memphis group Booker T. and the MGs: guitarist Steve Cropper, bassist Donald "Duck" Dunn, and keyboardist Booker T. Jones. Los Angeles, 1995**

# Jazz and the Blues

The blues and jazz are first cousins, though each has traveled along its own trajectory since exploding onto the music scene around the turn of the twentieth century. Their paths have often crossed, however, and many future jazz stars served their apprenticeships in blues-oriented bands, particularly during the rhythm and blues era. Virtually every jazz instrumentalist worth his or her salt—from Louis Armstrong and Sidney Bechet through Charlie Christian and Charlie Parker to Thelonious Monk and John Coltrane—has been a master of blues improvisation, and more than a few jazz singers have taken to twelve-bar blues as naturally as they have to pop tunes of the Tin Pan Alley and Broadway variety.

Louis Armstrong was the first great jazz virtuoso, his innovations of the 1920s and early 1930s profoundly altering the shape of American music to come. The New Orleans musician's multioctave trumpet (or cornet) solos soared with ravishing grandeur, and he virtually invented the art of jazz singing, including wordless scat. Among Armstrong's most stunning blues performances are "Gut Bucket Blues," "I'm Not Rough," "Savoy Blues," "West End Blues," and "Basin Street Blues," all cut between 1925 and 1928 with all-star studio groups billed as the Hot Five or Hot Seven. Many of these sides made ingenious use of breaks, stop-time, double-time, and other rhythmic devices that unfortunately were soon abandoned in both the jazz and blues idioms, although trumpeter Wynton Marsalis (also a New Orleans native) resurrected some of them six and a half decades later for such postmodern works as *The Majesty of the Blues* and *Soul Gestures in Southern Blue*. Armstrong also accompanied numerous blues singers in the studio during this period, among them classic blueswomen Bessie Smith and Bertha "Chippie" Hill, obscure country bluesman Nolan Welsh, and famous "Blue Yodeler" Jimmie Rodgers.

Texas trombonist Jack Teagarden was among Armstrong's foremost disciples, both as an instrumentalist and as a vocalist. Considered by many to have been the greatest of all white blues singers, Teagarden first recorded with Armstrong in 1929 and was a member of his mentor's combo from 1947 to 1951, during which time the two men performed such memorable duets as "Back o' Town Blues" and "Jack-Armstrong Blues." Another notable Armstrong-influenced singing instrumentalist who specialized in blues was trumpeter Oran "Hot Lips" Page, also a Texan.

As might be expected, blues has been particularly pronounced in the work of numerous jazz guitarists, from such early practitioners as Teddy Bunn, George

> I think if it wasn't for the blues, there wouldn't be no jazz.
>
> —T-Bone Walker

> He was the Prometheus of the blues idiom.... Everywhere [Louis] Armstrong went in the 1920s, he created a revolution in musical sensibility....His assimilation, elaboration, extensions, and refinement of its elements became in effect the touchstone for all who came after him.
>
> —Albert Murray,
> **writer**

OPPOSITE:
**Louis Armstrong was a beacon for just about everybody...instrumentalists and singers alike. London, 1985**

Barnes, Tiny Grimes, and brothers Oscar and Johnny Moore to modern stylists like Kenny Burrell, Billy Butler, George Benson, Melvin Sparks, and John Scofield. Although his recording career lasted only two years (1939–1941), Dallas-born, Oklahoma-bred guitarist Charlie Christian played an immense role in popularizing the then-novel electric guitar with a radical new style that presaged bebop. Christian, in the words of author Albert Murray, "not only mastered all of the soulful nuances of traditional blues-idiom statement but also made of the guitar a hornlike solo vehicle with orchestral rank equivalent to the trumpet, the trombone, and the saxophone."

A blues aesthetic, as well as the blues form itself, permeated the music of early jazz composers and pianists Jelly Roll Morton and Duke Ellington. During the swing era, which lasted roughly from 1935 to the end of World War II, nearly every big band had blues

numbers in its book, though some bands featured blues more prominently than others. Among the jazz orchestras in which blues was a major component were those of Count Basie, Jay McShann (from whose band emerged pioneering bebop alto saxophonist Charlie Parker), Lucky Millinder, Erskine Hawkins (whose 1940 recording of the slow blues "After Hours," featuring its composer, pianist Avery Parrish, was so popular that some called it "the Negro national anthem"), Lionel Hampton, Cootie Williams, and Buddy Johnson. Of the white big bands, clarinetist-saxophonist Woody Herman's had the strongest reputation for its blues performances.

Most of the black big bands had vocalists who specialized in blues or at least included some in their repertoires. Basie had Jimmy Rushing, Helen Humes, Billie Holiday (briefly), and, in the 1950s, Joe Williams. Walter Brown was McShann's star blues singer until Jimmy Witherspoon took his place. Blues-style gospel singer-guitarist Sister Rosetta Tharpe and blues shouter Wynonne Harris both passed through Millinder's ranks. Dinah Washington and Sonny Parker sang with Hampton, while Buddy Johnson featured his sister Ella along with Arthur Prysock. Among blues singers associated with jazz, but not with a specific band, were the great Joe Turner and his disabled disciple, Doc Pomus.

Blues was never far from the surface of the bebop movement of the mid-1940s and became increasingly pronounced in the mid-1950s hard bop of Horace Silver and in the soul-jazz of Cannonball Adderley and Les McCann. Bop pianist Ray Bryant displayed a particular affinity for older blues styles in such recordings as "Blues #3" and "Slow Freight," while idiosyncratic Mississippi-born singer-pianist Mose Allison incorporated tunes by bluesmen Willie Dixon, Mercy Dee Walton, Aleck "Sonny Boy Williamson" Miller, and Johnny Fuller into his repertoire. During

**Big band titans Duke Ellington and Cab Calloway at a _Life_ magazine party with Duke's singer Ivie Anderson and Keynote Records producer Harry Lim. New York City, 1939**

Billie Holiday's best blues recordings were in the 1930s and 1940s for Columbia and Commodore with top-flight jazz players as her accompanists. Holiday with guitarist Jimmy McLin. New York City, 1939

the 1980s, trombonist-arranger Jimmy Cheatham and his wife, singer-pianist Jeannie Cheatham, achieved wide popularity in jazz circles with their lively blues interpretations.

Perhaps the most strongly blues-informed style of modern jazz has evolved among Hammond B-3 organ players. The instrument gained a foothold during the early 1950s through the work of Wild Bill Davis and Bill Doggett (a former Lucky Millinder and Louis Jordan sideman whose 1956 recording of "Honky Tonk" was the biggest rhythm and blues instrumental hit of that decade), but really took off mid-decade through Philadelphia organist Jimmy Smith's innovative, hard-swinging mix of blues and bop.

Jimmy Smith inspired a legion of followers, including Jack McDuff, Richard "Groove" Holmes,

Johnny "Hammond" Smith, Lonnie Smith, Charles Earland, and the bluesiest of them all, Jimmy McGriff. Organ groups were popular attractions at cocktail lounges in African-American communities throughout the United States during the 1960s; among other musicians closely associated with the idiom are saxophonists Stanley Turrentine, Lou Donaldson, Hank Crawford, Houston Person, and Grover Washington, Jr., and guitarists Bill Jennings, George Benson, Boogaloo Joe Jones, Melvin Sparks, and O'Donel Levy.

Organ jazz had fallen from favor by the mid-1970s, but eventually reemerged in trendy London clubs in the late 1980s under a new name—acid jazz—and eventually became something of a fad among young, hip, urban Americans. The blue side of jazz had come back home.

JAZZ AND THE BLUES

Trumpeter Cootie Williams' plunger-mute growl technique was a significant element in the Duke Ellington band's blues performances. Boston, 1958

Mississippi native Mose
Allison composes and
sings rural as well as very
sophisticated urban blues.
Provincetown,
Massachusetts, 1964

ABOVE:

The legendary trom-
bonist and blues
singer Jack Teagarden
worked with Louis
Armstrong in
1929...then again in
the 1940s and 1950s.
Chicago, 1956

RIGHT:
**Lionel Hampton's
blues-drenched
band featured some
of the best blues
sax players, including
Arnett Cobb, Illinois
Jacquet, Johnny
Griffin, and
Herbie Fields.
New York City, 1946**

ABOVE:
**Dinah Washington started as a blues singer
with Lionel Hampton's mid-1940s band.
New York City, 1954**

OPPOSITE:
**An all-star quartet at the Open Door in
Greenwich Village, including Thelonious Monk
on piano, Charlie Parker on alto sax, Charles
Mingus on bass, and Roy Haynes on drums.
All four were deeply rooted in the blues.
New York City, 1953**

Milt Jackson is a
vibraharp master
of bop, ballads, and,
most definitely,
the blues.
Emeryville, California,
1992

Pianist Avery Parrish's playing of the blues "After Hours" was an enormous hit for trumpeter Erskine Hawkins' band. Boston, 1959

Powerful trumpet player and earthy blues singer "Hot Lips" Page with New Orleans blues master Sidney Bechet at Ryan's on Manhattan's "Swing Street," West Fifty-second Street. New York City, 1941

ABOVE:
**Lucky Millinder's band featured gospel singer Sister Rosetta Tharpe, who also played superb blues guitar. New York City, 1942**

OPPOSITE:
**Jimmy McGriff is the bluesiest of all the jazz organ players. Boston, 1966**

ABOVE:
**Jimmy Smith plays a hard-swinging mix of blues and bop. Emeryville, California, 1992**

# Folk Blues

Veteran folklorist John A. Lomax and his eighteen-year-old son, Alan, hit a gold mine during the summer of 1933 while traveling through Texas and Louisiana in search of songs to publish in a book to be titled *American Ballads and Folk Songs*. At Angola State Penitentiary in Louisiana, they were entertained by one Huddie Ledbetter—better known as Leadbelly—who was serving time for assault with intent to commit murder. The Lomaxes were immediately impressed with Leadbelly's powerful baritone voice, his rhythmically propulsive twelve-string guitar playing, and particularly his vast repertoire of songs, including topical ballads, work songs, spirituals, and blues. They set up their state-of-the-art 315-pound (143kg) disc-cutting machine and proceeded to record Leadbelly performing such numbers as "Angola Blues" and a sentimental waltz that came to be known as "Goodnight, Irene."

The twelve-inch aluminum discs having been deposited at the Library of Congress, the father-and-son team returned to Angola a year later to record more and to help secure the singer's release. John Lomax soon became Leadbelly's manager, and Leadbelly became Lomax's client, chauffeur, and occasional cook. The folklorist brought Leadbelly north and secured informal concert and commercial recording dates for him, but Lomax proved to be a highly domineering manager, tightly controlling the singer's money and insisting, for the sake of "authenticity," that Leadbelly perform in coveralls rather than in the double-breasted suits he favored.

Although Leadbelly soon fell out with John Lomax (though he remained close to Alan), he'd arrived in New York City at the beginning of a folk revival initiated by a group of Communists and their allies who were looking for authentic proletarian folksingers as a counterbalance to the pop music coming out of capitalist Tin Pan Alley. Championed by *Daily Worker* journalists Mike Gold and Richard Wright, Leadbelly found himself at the center of a loose alliance of left-leaning artists that included folksingers Aunt Molly Jackson, Burl Ives, Woody Guthrie, and Pete Seeger; blues singers Josh White, Sonny Terry, and Brownie McGhee; actor Will Geer; and concert singer and actor Paul Robeson.

Leadbelly died of Lou Gehrig's disease in 1949, and McCarthyism drove the final nail into the coffin of the Left's folk revival shortly thereafter. White intellectuals, however, still longed for blues singers whose music remained "pure," that is, uncorrupted by commercialism and modernity. Mississippi-born singer-guitarist Big Bill Broonzy, a major Chicago blues star of the 1930s, stepped in to fill the role, trading his suits for overalls and his swinging urban blues style

> More than any other black folk-blues artist of his time, Leadbelly helped expose his race's vast musical riches to white America, and, in the process, helped preserve a folk legacy that has become a significant part of this nation's musical treasury.
>
> —Robert Santelli,
> **writer**

for a repertoire of folk songs, spirituals, and exaggerated country blues. White audiences ate up this pseudo-authenticity, especially in western Europe, where Broonzy toured regularly from 1951 until his death in 1958. His popularity there created overseas opportunities for other U.S. bluesmen—Muddy Waters, Willie Dixon, and Memphis Slim among the first—and helped to spawn the skiffle music movement in England (perhaps best exemplified by Lonnie Donegan's hit 1956 version of Leadbelly's "Rock Island Line"), which in turn influenced bands like the Beatles and the Rolling Stones.

**Bob Dylan's switch to amplification in 1965 signaled the beginning of the end of the second folk revival. Copenhagen, 1966**

Broonzy had cultivated the myth that he was the last of the country blues singers, and for many fans, his passing marked the end of an era. This notion was put to rest the following year, however, with the publication of Samuel Charters' book *The Country Blues* and the release by Folkways (Leadbelly's old label) of Texas bluesman Lightnin' Hopkins' first album. What followed was a rush to record every and any acoustic artist who might appeal to the new market of college students and young intellectuals who'd been primed for folk music by the Kingston Trio.

"Within ten years of Leadbelly's death," author Stephen Calt once observed, "'folk' music had erupted as a popular alternative to rock and roll. To its growing constituency of the late 1950s and early 1960s, folk music was noncommercial music, redolent of a hand-crafted rather than mass-produced product, the work of humans instead of a machine."

The 1960s were the golden age of folk-blues. Dozens of largely forgotten blues artists were tracked down and signed to newly hatched record labels like Arhoolie, Bluesville, and Delmark. Among the many veterans who found their careers rejuvenated by the folk-blues boom were Pink Anderson, Sleepy John Estes, Son House, Mississippi John Hurt, Skip James, Lonnie Johnson, Furry Lewis, Bukka White, and Big Joe Williams. Sonny Terry and Brownie McGhee, veterans of the earlier folk revival, became the most successful duo of the new one. Other important country blues stylists such as Mance Lipscomb, Mississippi Fred McDowell, and Robert Pete Williams made their professional debuts during the period. And, on occasion, electric blues giants like Muddy Waters and John Lee Hooker would even unplug to satiate the folk purists.

Inspired by the ragtimelike blues guitar picking of Reverend Gary Davis, a number of young white musicians took to acoustic blues, among them Roy Bookbinder, Stefan Grossman, Dave Van Ronk, and Bob Dylan (whose switch to amplified music at the 1965 Newport Folk Festival, where he was backed by the Butterfield Blues Band, signaled the beginning of the end of the second folk revival). Other notable white folk-blues artists who emerged during the era included Rory Block, John Hammond, Jr., Geoff Muldaur, and Eric Von Schmidt. Folk singer Odetta, Reverend Davis disciple Larry Johnson, and the daringly eclectic Taj Mahal were among the very few young African-American musicians to achieve prominence during the folk-blues movement of the 1960s. It wasn't until later—in the mid-1970s with the duo of John Cephas and Phil Wiggins, and in the mid-1990s with Corey Harris, Alvin Youngblood Hart, and Keb' Mo'—that other young black men emerged to reclaim the folk roots of the blues on their own terms.

RIGHT:
"To Mr. [John] Hurt the guitar was less an instrument than it was a partner in a two-member group."
(Robert Shelton, writer)
Newport, Rhode Island, 1968

ABOVE:
Reverend Gary Davis had a ragtime-like guitar style.
Newport, Rhode Island, 1968

RIGHT:
Keb' Mo' commented, "In my lyrics, I try to talk about universal feelings.... We need to treat each other like we want to be treated.... I try to uplift. It is what I aspire to."
Berwyn, Illinois, 1996

FOLK BLUES

ABOVE:

"Skip James was a complete original... [his intense] melismatic falsetto...[was] an upper register shiver that we today associate with love's rapture or the soul's deliverance." (Francis Davis, writer)
Paris, 1967

RIGHT:

Rediscovered by record producer Bob Koester, a near-blind Sleepy John Estes spent his final years as a coffeehouse favorite, particularly in Chicago, but continued to make his home in rural Tennessee.
Chicago, 1971

Classic blues singer
Sippie Wallace, backed
by Jim Kweskin's Jug
Band, the group that
launched the careers
of Geoff and Maria
Muldaur.
Newport, Rhode
Island, 1968

"Taj Mahal [is] one of the few black hands-on [blues] preservationists, a likable eclectic whose interpretations of older blues songs and originals...[are] ingratiatingly eccentric, if sometimes a trifle bookish." (Francis Davis, writer) Boston, 1968

ABOVE:

**"Big Joe Williams' churning twelve-string guitar...and dark-tempered vocals...always sounding like a misplaced Delta sharecropper.... The angry power of his music was such that even at his most freewheeling, he sounded like someone or something had just rubbed him the wrong way." (Francis Davis, writer) Chicago, 1962**

LEFT:

**John Hammond, Jr., has said, "I felt when I started playing I had my own voice and my own way of playing and feeling things." Cambridge, Massachusetts, 1965**

# The Rhythm and Blues Era

The term "rhythm and blues" was coined in 1949 by Jerry Wexler, then a staff writer for *Billboard*. Wexler later became an executive and producer at Atlantic Records, a company that played an important role in the development of the genre. Although the abbreviation R&B is still widely used, particularly in music industry circles, to categorize all African-American popular music (even rap), rhythm and blues more specifically applies to the blues-oriented music with a strong beat that was in vogue between the end of the swing era and the triumph of soul—from the late 1940s to around 1960.

Bandleader Johnny Otis, a former jazz drummer who became one of the major R&B stars of the early 1950s, eloquently outlined the economic, sociological, and musical forces that gave rise to rhythm and blues at the end of World War II: "My case is kinda typical, along with Joe Liggins, Roy Milton, Sonny Thompson, T-Bone Walker, and a few others. We all had big band experience, and we all longed for that big band sound, but the day came and the money wasn't there. People's tastes changed; the war was over and the economy took a big tumble. We were faced with having to survive in music, so I did what a lot of us did. Instead of seven or eight brass, I cut down to two brass, and instead of five reeds, I cut it down to two reeds." Otis also selected "a twangy,

T-Bone Walker–type" guitar player, a pianist who specialized in blues and boogie woogies, and a drummer who could maintain a heavy, unflagging backbeat.

"I had noticed in the years previous with my big band that while the people loved jazz, they really came to life when we played 'After Hours' or boogie woogies or jumps," Otis said. "That's what really moved them, so when I started recording with the smaller band, I moved in that direction and so did the other guys. It was a commercial move. We began a synthesis of bringing together swing big band flavors, country blues, a touch of gospel, and even a little bebop from time to time. That's how rhythm and blues was born."

Arkansas-born singer and alto saxophonist Louis Jordan, himself a veteran of Chick Webb's jazz orchestra, had already laid much of the stylistic groundwork for rhythm and blues. Backed by a riff-based shuffle-boogie combo called the Tympany Five, Jordan was the most popular African-American recording artist of the 1940s. Uptempo, humor-laced Jordan numbers like "Caldonia," "Choo Choo Ch'Boogie," "Ain't Nobody Here But Us Chickens," and "Saturday Night Fish Fry" proved as popular with whites as they did with black people.

While Jordan recorded for the well-entrenched Decca label, the vast majority of subsequent rhythm

> For a long time the blues purists were suspicious of Louis Jordan, simply because he had been successful….The same type of response is commonplace in the jazz world…but they gradually came to realize what a seminal figure he was in the development of their music.
>
> —John Chilton, writer

**OPPOSITE:**
**Louis Jordan laid the stylistic groundwork for R&B.
New York City, 1946**

**Hank Ballard, leader of the Midnighters, composed and recorded the original version of "The Twist." Newport, Rhode Island, 1996**

and blues artists rose to fame on independent labels that emerged after the war—Apollo, Aristocrat/Chess, Atlantic, DeLuxe, Duke/Peacock, Exclusive, Juke Box/Specialty, Modern/RPM, Queen/King, Philo/Aladdin, Savoy, and Swingtime, to name the most prominent. Rhythm and blues artists were answering the demand for blues and gospel music that had been largely abandoned by the major companies due to wartime shellac shortages. Unlike Decca, which could get Louis Jordan songs played on white pop stations, the indies had few such connections, and early stars of rhythm and blues like Johnny Ace, Charles Brown, Fats Domino, the Drifters, the 5 Royales, Lowell Fulson, Guitar Slim, John Lee Hooker, Ivory Joe Hunter, Roy Brown, Bullmoose Jackson, B.B. King, Joe Liggins, the Dominoes, Little Esther, Percy Mayfield, Ruth Brown, the Midnighters, Amos Milburn, Roy Milton, Johnny Otis, Lloyd Price, the Ravens, Willie Mae "Big Mama" Thornton, and Muddy Waters were thus largely unknown outside the African-American community.

It had long been a regular record-industry practice for a company to have one of its artists "cover" a hit tune by an artist on another label in hopes of cashing in on some of the profits or, better yet, gaining a market edge over the original. The cover game took on a particularly odious racial tinge during the early 1950s as one R&B hit after another was copied by a white artist (usually for a major label) who ended up getting the bulk of the sales because the black artist who'd done the original couldn't get played on pop radio. Notorious examples include Bill Haley and the Comets' Decca version of Joe Turner's Atlantic hit "Shake, Rattle, and Roll" (the group's producer, Milt Gabler, had produced Louis Jordan a decade earlier) and Pat Boone's various Milquetoast treatments of Fats Domino, Ivory Joe Hunter, and Little Richard tunes. Sometimes, as in the case of white pop singer Georgia Gibbs' cover of Atlantic artist LaVern Baker's "Tweedle Dee," the same studio, engineer, and musicians were used to duplicate the sound of the original. (Incensed, Baker lobbied Congress to enact a bill protecting musical arrangements. The law failed to pass, but Baker maintained a sense of humor about the situation, once quipping that, when flying, she'd take out insurance in Gibbs' name so "she'd be covered in case something happened to me.")

Radio's racial barriers began coming down in a big way around 1955, when rhythm and blues performers like Baker, Chuck Berry, the Coasters, Fats Domino, Little Richard, Ivory Joe Hunter, and Lloyd Price started showing up on the pop charts alongside Pat Boone, Bill Haley, and Elvis Presley as rock and roll fever swept the United States and soon the world. Rock and roll appeared to be rhythm and blues' salvation, and for a period the two genres were virtually indistinguishable. By the end of the 1950s, however, much of rock had shed its blues underpinnings as it moved closer to the mainstream. Concurrently, R&B artists like Ray Charles, Little Willie John, and Sam Cooke began injecting heavy doses of gospel into their music, and rhythm and blues gave way to soul in the popular consciousness.

LEFT:

**Willie Mae "Big Mama" Thornton recorded the original version of "Hound Dog."**
**New York City, 1983**

LEFT:

**From age thirteen until her death at forty-eight, Little Esther Phillips recorded a remarkable body of music, from straight blues and jumpin' R&B to country, soul, jazz, and disco material.**
**New York City, 1980**

ABOVE:

**Billed as "Little Miss Sharecropper" early in her career, Lavern Baker was one of the first R&B singers to be embraced by rock and roll audiences.**
**New York City, 1990**

ABOVE:
**The hard-pumping, blues-based sides Little Richard recorded for Specialty Records in the mid-1950s represent rock and roll at its most incendiary.**
**Los Angeles, 1994**

OPPOSITE:
**Ray Charles is a towering figure of twentieth century music, having achieved mass popularity with his ingenious synthesis of blues, gospel, jazz, country, and Tin Pan Alley traditions.**
**New York City, 1993**

# Rock (and Roll)

There was a relatively brief period, roughly from 1955 to 1963, when the racial, regional, and stylistic walls that had traditionally segregated American popular music came tumbling down. Take, for instance, a week from late fall 1957, when such diverse records as Elvis Presley's blues-flavored rocker "Jailhouse Rock," the sentimental movie sound-track song "Tammy" by Debbie Reynolds, Texas country singer Ray Price's western swing weeper "My Shoes Keep Walking Back to You," shouter Bobby Bland's intense Texas blues shuffle "Farther Up the Road," and the smooth Sam Cooke R&B ballad "You Send Me" were being programmed concurrently on the nation's pop radio stations. This new openness coincided with the advent of rock and roll and ended around the time of the genre's second, British wave, after which program directors and the consultants on which they relied for wisdom came to the conclusion, allegedly based on market research, that maximum ratings could be achieved by segregating the sounds all over again. Rock even lost its "roll" and, with it, its black component, with a few notable exceptions such as Jimi Hendrix and Lenny Kravitz.

The term "rock and roll" was coined in 1951 by Alan Freed, a white disc jockey in Cleveland, Ohio, who was consciously aiming black rhythm and blues records at a white teen audience. If we are to believe Billy Ward, who claims to have been present in the studio at that moment, Freed got the idea from a line sung by basso Bill Brown—"I rock 'em, roll 'em, all night long"—in "Sixty-Minute Man," a massive (and decidedly sexual) rhythm and blues hit by Ward's singing group, the Dominoes.

"Freed leaped to his feet," Ward recalled. "'That's it,' he cried hoarsely. 'Rock and roll! That's what it is.' Immediately he broadcast his name for our sound. And all the trade publications fell in line with his thinking."

For some, rock and roll was merely an alternate name for rhythm and blues, and many R&B performers benefited greatly from the new crossover exposure, particularly blues-based stylists Fats Domino and the flamboyant Little Richard. For the more musicologically inclined, however, rock and roll represents a unique fusion of the blues and country strains of U.S. popular music and is perhaps best exemplified by the early work of Elvis Presley and Chuck Berry.

Presley's first record, done for Sun Records in Memphis on July 6, 1954, had a rhythm-charged arrangement of bluegrass pioneer Bill Monroe's "Blue Moon of Kentucky" on one side and a souped-up treatment of Mississippi bluesman Arthur "Big Boy" Crudup's "That's All Right" on the other. Over the next two years, Presley would record two more Crudup tunes, "My Baby Left Me" and "So Glad You're Mine," along with blues numbers associated with Roy Brown, Arthur Gunter, and Little Junior Parker. Presley included

> We're talking about an interracial relationship with country music that produced twins, a black boy named Chuck and a white boy named Elvis.... It isn't enough to say that Elvis treated thousands of white teenagers to their first sugared taste of black music....That's not giving him his proper due. He was one of the finest white blues singers...one of the finest singers ever spawned by the Southern United States.
> —Francis Davis,
> **writer**

OPPOSITE:
**"Elvis Presley, the white man who most successfully and joyously 'went native' by bringing black pop rhythms into adolescent mass America."
(Stanley Crouch, writer)
Tippo, Mississippi, 1957**

Influential stylist and spokesperson Chuck Berry was inspired by T-Bone Walker. Brussels, 1965

blues in his repertoire throughout his career, though they began losing their edge after he started recording for RCA Victor in 1956.

If Presley was the king of rock and roll, Berry was the genre's most influential stylist and articulate spokesperson, poetically proclaiming its arrival in such blues-based anthems as "Roll Over Beethoven" and "Rock and Roll Music." Inspired by guitarists T-Bone Walker and Carl Hogan (of Louis Jordan's Tympany Five), Berry also listened to country music while he was growing up in St. Louis. "Maybellene," his first record, cut for Chess Records in Chicago on May 21, 1955, was a reworking of the hillbilly hoedown standard "Ida Red." The flip side was a slow blues titled "Wee Wee Hours."

That Berry's brand of rock and roll was distinct from the rhythm and blues mainstream is borne out by the fact that it had minimal impact on the styles of black R&B artists who followed in his wake, while its influence on white rockers on both sides of the Atlantic—from Lonnie Mack, the Beach Boys, and Creedence Clearwater Revival in the United States to the Beatles, the Rolling Stones, the Yardbirds, and countless other bands in England—was profound.

The electric blues movement in England was launched during the early 1960s by guitarist Alexis Korner and harmonica player Cyril Davies, who quickly attracted an array of followers that included Charlie Watts, Jack Bruce, Mick Jagger, Keith Richards, Brian Jones, Eric Burdon, Rod Stewart, Jimmy Page, and Jeff Beck. While many early British blues enthusiasts gravitated toward the world of rock, John Mayall maintained a more authentic blues approach with his Blues Breakers, which briefly included former Yardbirds guitarist Eric Clapton and spawned the careers of Mick Fleetwood and John McVie, who together with Peter Green and Jeremy Spencer, launched the original blues

edition of Fleetwood Mac. The origins of heavy metal can be traced to the high-decibel, blues-imbued rock of such British bands as Cream (featuring Clapton), the Jimi Hendrix Experience (although Hendrix was from the United States, the trio was formed in England), and Led Zeppelin (featuring Jimmy Page).

A similar electric blues-rock movement developed in the United States during the mid-1960s, the primary domestic catalyst being the high-energy Chicago blues of the Butterfield Blues Band. The group, which featured guitarists Michael Bloomfield and Elvin Bishop, greatly influenced a generation of musicians, including such rock bands as Jefferson Airplane, the Grateful Dead, and Santana. Other prominent American blues-rock artists include Canned Heat, the Steve Miller Band (the first edition of which featured singer-guitarist Boz Scaggs), Roy Buchanan, the Allman Brothers Band, brothers Johnny and Edgar Winter, ZZ Top, and the raw and raucous George Thorogood and the Destroyers.

**Checker Records mates Bo "I'm a Man" Diddley and Koko "I'm a Woman" Taylor backstage. Chicago, 1994**

ROCK (AND ROLL)

ABOVE:
**"In the 1950s teenage boys had dreamed of singing like Elvis. By the late 1960s...teenage boys were itching to spew licks like [guitarist] Jeff Beck (shown here) or Jimmy Page or Eric Clapton and to form their own bands." (Francis Davis, writer) New York City, 1977**

OPPOSITE:
**Janis Joplin was a [blues] preservationist by virtue of her conscious debts to Bessie Smith and "Big Mama" Thornton. Newport, Rhode Island, 1968**

# Soul Blues

THE MUSIC OF THE AFRICAN-AMERICAN CHURCH HAS LONG informed the blues—and vice versa. "Blues is so close to religious music that you can play a blues in the church now and they think's one of them good old swingin' hymns," bluesman Lowell Fulson once observed. "A song is a song," soul and blues singer Johnnie Taylor once stated. "If you sing 'Jesus' or you sing 'baby,' it's basically melodically the same. I think anything that makes people happy is good, anything that takes people's minds off their problems."

Some early blues artists, such as Blind Lemon Jefferson, Charley Patton, and Skip James, recorded religious numbers on the side, usually under a pseudonym. The legendary father of gospel, Thomas A. Dorsey, (as Georgia Tom) popularized risqué blues numbers like "It's Tight Like That" during the late 1920s but soon after abandoned the blues altogether and, using techniques learned from his blues experience, played a founding role in gospel music. Among Dorsey's best-known gospel compositions are "Take My Hand, Precious Lord," "There'll Be Peace in the Valley for Me," and "Search Me, Lord."

Modern blues titans B.B. King and Bobby Bland were greatly influenced by prominent gospel quartet lead singers—King by Sam McCrary of the Fairfield Four, Bland by Ira Tucker of the Dixie Hummingbirds—while such protosoul singers as Roy Brown and Clyde McPhatter drew inspiration from the same deep well.

The spiritual and secular strains of African-American vernacular music collided head-on during the mid-1950s and fused to form the basis of what would be dubbed soul music. Ray Charles blended the two genres by applying chord progressions, rhythms, and call-and-response patterns borrowed from Alex Bradford, James Cleveland, and other gospel artists to his incendiary blues-style vocal performances. Others, particularly vocalists Little Willie John and Ted Taylor, took a converse course, superimposing gospel phrasing, particularly its syllable-splitting melismas, over twelve-bar blues chord changes. It is this second approach, most commonly associated with singers for whom blues is only a part of their repertoire, that has come to be called soul-blues.

> I think the blues is always a part of this [soul] music.
> —Johnnie Taylor

"Part Time Love," recorded in 1963 by Little Johnny Taylor, is the quintessential soul-blues record. The Los Angeles–based singer had been in gospel quartets, including an early edition of the soon-to-be-famous Mighty Clouds of Joy, when he was a teenager before falling under the spell of Little Willie John and Ted Taylor and switching to rhythm and blues. With his fervent, melisma-dripping reading of "Part Time Love," Little Johnny offered a refreshingly modern, intensely soulful take on the blues during a period when the blues were rapidly passing from popular fashion in the African-American community. The song shot to the top of *Billboard*'s R&B chart and became the best-selling blues record of the 1960s.

Another Los Angeles–based former gospel singer, whose name happened to be Johnnie Taylor, eventually gained the upper hand over Little Johnny.

**OPPOSITE:**
**Former gospel singer Johnnie Taylor was known as "The Blues Wailer" during the 1960s.**
**New York City, 1991**

Johnnie, who'd replaced Sam Cooke in the Sould Stirrers after Cooke's 1957 switch from sacred to secular music, followed in his friend's footsteps a few years later and began recording soul and blues numbers for Cooke's Derby and SAR record labels. But while Cooke cut an occasional twelve-bar blues (1963's "Little Red Rooster" being the most successful), Johnnie made blues a key component of his repertoire, especially after he added "Part Time Love" to his nightclub repertoire and set out on a cross-country tour, causing considerable confusion with audiences as he cashed in on the other singer's success. After signing with Stax Records in Memphis in 1966, Johnnie had a string of similarly styled soul-blues hits of his own, including "I've Got to Love Somebody's Baby" and "Somebody's Sleeping in My Bed," but largely abandoned the style after achieving massive popularity with such up-tempo soul smashes as "Who's Making Love" and "Disco Lady." Stax continued perfecting its soul-blues production style, however, achieving especially winning results with singer-guitarists Albert King and Little Milton.

The blues innovations of Stax staff producers Isaac Hayes, David Porter, Booker T. Jones, Steve Cropper, and Al Jackson, Jr.—along with those of rival Memphis producer Willie Mitchell in his work with O.V. Wright, Ann Peebles, Al Green, and Otis Clay—set a stylistic tone for soul-blues that has remained dominant into the present era, particularly in the music of singer-guitarist Robert Cray and of artists who record for the Malaco label in Jackson, Mississippi.

This subgenre, the last type of blues to hold substantial commercial currency in the African-American community, suffered a huge dip in popularity when black-oriented radio stations across the country, following the lead of Nashville's powerful WLAC (which once billed itself as "Blues Radio"), dropped blues records from their playlists during the mid-1970s. Black radio was devoid of blues during the disco era, except as filtered through the funk of such blues-rooted guitar pickers as Johnny "Guitar" Watson (who said he was giving the blues "a shot of first aid"), Leroy "Sugarfoot" Bonner of the Ohio Players, and Roger Troutman of Zapp.

Journeyman soul-blues singer Z.Z. Hill, who, like Johnnie Taylor, had turned his back on the blues when disco was in vogue, returned to the genre in 1982 with his Malaco recording of "Down Home Blues." Although it wasn't released as a single, the track captured the imagination of radio programmers and the public. The first blues to receive substantial airplay on black radio in nearly a decade, it became the blues anthem of the 1980s and established Hill as a star on the so-called chitlin circuit until his death in 1984. Malaco gradually cornered the soul-blues market, building an impressive artist roster that includes Denise LaSalle, Bobby Bland, Little Milton, Latimore, Tyrone Davis, Bobby Rush, Artie "Blues Boy" White, and even Johnnie Taylor, whose Malaco albums invariably contain a blues or two.

Oddly, due to record company marketing practices and booking agency affiliations, Malaco artists are largely unknown outside the African-American community, while the similarly styled Robert Cray (whose career took off in the mid-1980s after he was championed by Mick Jagger, Eric Clapton, and other rock stars) has an overwhelmingly white constituency, as do such other soul-blues performers as Etta James, Irma Thomas, Otis Clay, Ann Peebles, and Joe Louis Walker.

> In some ways, soul simply replaced the blues. Motown was black pop....But soul as exemplified by Ray Charles, Aretha Franklin, Otis Redding, Al Green, and early James Brown was another story: pop more urgently contemporary than Motown, but as downhome in dialect and frame of reference.
> —Francis Davis,
> **writer**

ABOVE:
**James Brown record-
ed a number of blues
songs during his first
decade as the hardest
working man in show
business.
New York City, 1986**

RIGHT:
**Little Milton imitated
B.B. King and Bobby
Bland early in his
career but developed
a distinctive soul-
blues style in the
mid-1960s.
New York City, 1990**

LEFT:
**The career of soul singer Denise LaSalle took off after she embraced the blues in the early 1980s. Chicago, 1994**

OPPOSITE:
**"Dr. Feelgood" and other blues songs are part of soul queen Aretha Franklin's repertoire. Boston, 1965**

RIGHT:
**Irma Thomas is known as "The Queen of New Orleans Soul." New York City, 1992**

**Robert Cray helped
jump-start interest
in the blues in the
1980s with his innov-
ative guitar work and
soul-soaked vocals.
New Orleans, 1991**

**Deejay, dancer, and
vocalist Rufus
Thomas, the senior
citizen of Memphis
soul.
New York City, 1991**

SOUL BLUES

114

Etta James stated, "I wanna show that gospel, country, blues, rhythm and blues, jazz, rock 'n' roll are all just really one thing. Those are the American music and that is the American culture."
Chicago, 1993

# GUITARISTS

THE GUITAR AND THE BLUES HAVE BEEN INEXORABLY LINKED SINCE the music's birth. Although the banjo and, to a lesser extent the fiddle, were also widely employed by early blues musicians, the guitar had become the genre's dominant instrument by the 1920s and became increasingly so over the next seven decades. The banjo may have been of African origin, but the Spanish guitar proved better suited to the new music being created by Africans in North America.

Critic Robert Palmer once pointed out that "the African instruments with the most highly developed solo traditions tend to be instruments like the widely distributed hand piano or the harplike lutes of Senegambia that can simultaneously produce driving ostinatos [repeated patterns] and chording or melody lines that answer or comment on the player's singing. The persistence of this principle in America helps explain the alacrity with which black musicians in the rural South took up the guitar once white musicians and mail-order catalogues introduced it to them."

Lonnie Johnson played banjo, fiddle, guitar, mandolin, bass, piano, and harmonium while growing up in New Orleans during the twentieth century's first two decades, but he eventually settled on guitar, and it is as a guitarist that Johnson's reputation looms as the father of both the modern jazz and modern blues guitar traditions. His fluid single-string approach to soloing and sophisticated harmonic and rhythmic sense left a profound mark on several generations of guitar players, including Eddie Lang, Memphis Minnie, Blind Willie McTell, Brownie McGhee, Teddy Bunn, George Barnes, Charlie Christian, T-Bone Walker, Lowell Fulson, and B.B. King. Even the well-established finger-picking virtuoso Blind Blake and the soon-to-be-mythical Mississippi Delta bluesman Robert Johnson showed occasional traces of Lonnie's influence in their work. During the late 1920s, when Lonnie was much in demand for recording sessions, he was as comfortable accompanying "primitive" country blues singer Texas Alexander as he was in the faster musical company of the Duke Ellington Orchestra and Louis Armstrong's Hot Five.

> [Lonnie Johnson] remains to this day one of the originals, uniquely both a first-generation bluesman and jazzman...an innovator and model musician whose authorship of modern blues guitar alone would guarantee his position in the history of American music.
> —James Sallis, writer

According to historian James Sallis, Lonnie Johnson "is the major transitional figure in American guitar. Everything that came before—the complex patterns of Papa Charlie Jackson on six-string banjo, the ragtime blues of Blind Blake, the idiosyncratic runs and melodic flexibility of Blind Lemon Jefferson—comes together in his playing; and much that follows issues from it, right up to the jazz lines of Kenny Burrell or B.B. King's whiplike call-and-response guitar accompaniment."

By the time Johnson switched from acoustic to electric guitar in 1947, the amplified instrument had been in use for about a decade. Studio musician

OPPOSITE:
**Lonnie Johnson, a powerful influence on jazz and blues guitarists, started playing banjo, then fiddle and piano, but settled on guitar. Englewood Cliffs, New Jersey, 1960**

George Barnes (backing Big Bill Broonzy and other Chicago-based blues singers) and steel guitarists Floyd Smith (with Andy Kirk's jazz orchestra) and Frank Pasley (backing vocalist T-Bone Walker, who did not play on the session) were among the first to record blues on plugged-in models, but it was "Mean Old World," Walker's 1942 debut recording as an electric guitarist, that really opened the floodgates for electric blues.

Like the branches and leaves of a tree, all the major stylistic strains of electric blues guitar can be traced directly to T-Bone Walker's influence. Among blues guitar players who, like Walker, were based in California, Lowell Fulson, Pee Wee Crayton, Pete Lewis (with the Johnny Otis band), Jimmy Nolen (with Otis and later James Brown), Lafayette Thomas (with Jimmy McCracklin), and Johnny Heartsman became important Walker-rooted stylists in their own right. In Texas, Clarence "Gatemouth" Brown fashioned a brittle-toned take on the Walker sound that in turn influenced Johnny "Guitar" Watson and Albert Collins, both of whom, like Brown, used capos on the necks of their guitars and assumed gunslinger stances while playing. Collins, who was billed as "the Master of the Telecaster," inspired disciples of his own, notably Robert Cray, Bobby Murray, and Coco Montoya.

Eddie "Guitar Slim" Jones came up with a simplified yet dramatic version of the Walker style for his 1952 hit, "Things I Used to Do." Chuck Berry sped up some of Walker's trademark licks and used them as the basis for his own highly pervasive rock and roll style. And Wayne Bennett developed a remarkably complex Walker-inspired approach, of which his exquisitely subtle playing on Bobby Bland's 1962 version of Walker's "Call It Stormy Monday" is the most famous example. In recent years, Duke Robillard,

Ronnie Earl, and Rusty Zinn have been prominent torchbearers of the Walker legacy.

B.B. King, whose own early 1960s recording of "Mean Old World" is modeled on Walker's original, added a radical new dimension to Walker's innovations through the use of finger trills, string bending, and controlled amplifier feedback to create searing sustains. Beginning with his hit 1951 recording of Lowell Fulson's "Three O'Clock Blues," King became the most consistently successful bluesman of all time and spawned a legion of vocal and guitar disciples. Among a long list of guitarists who have displayed a pronounced B.B. King influence—not all of them strictly blues players—are Luther Allison, Mickey Baker, Elvin Bishop, Michael Bloomfield, Lonnie Brooks, Eric Clapton, Robben Ford, Freddie King, Roy Gaines, Peter Green, Buddy Guy, Pat Hare, Jimi Hendrix, Albert King, Little Milton, Magic Sam, Fenton Robinson, Otis Rush, Carlos Santana, John Scofield, Jimmy King, Melvin Sparks, Mick Taylor, Stevie Ray Vaughan, Johnny Winter, and Mighty Joe Young.

Slide (or bottleneck) guitar—which has its roots in the Mississippi Delta country blues of such artists as Charley Patton, Son House, and Robert Johnson and which was popularized in pre–World War II urban blues by Tampa Red—is a stylistic strain largely separate from the Lonnie Johnson/T-Bone Walker/B.B. King continuum. Notable electric slide guitarists include bluesman Elmore James, Muddy Waters, J.B. Hutto, and Hound Dog Taylor, as well as blues-rocker Duane Allman and the eclectic Ry Cooder.

The Hawaiian steel guitar, though capable of producing even more shimmering tonal qualities than the slide, has been largely absent in modern blues. Its few practitioners, all of them unjustly obscure, include L.C. Robinson, Hop Wilson, Sonny Rhodes, and Freddie Roulette.

**"Tiny Grimes was one of the earliest jazz electric guitarists to be influenced by Charlie Christian and he developed his own bluish swinging style." (Scott Yanow, writer) Hackensack, New Jersey, 1958**

LEFT:
**Texan Freddie King made his reputation in Chicago. Chicago, 1969**

ABOVE:
**"Jazzman Herb Ellis is at his best in a blues context...because of his depth and blues-driven swing...the joy and energy of his improvisations." (Nat Hentoff, writer) Emeryville, California, 1992**

LEFT:
**Texas guitarists Johnny Copeland (left) and Stevie Ray Vaughan (right) in concert. New York City, 1985**

LEFT:

"Although Jimi Hendrix will be remembered as rock's most innovative and revolutionary guitarist, he had the natural instincts of a bluesman and, in fact, built much of his early repertoire from the blues."
(Robert Santelli, writer)
Paris, 1967

OPPOSITE RIGHT:
**Magic Sam died
before he could
develop his full
potential.
Chicago, 1968**

BELOW:
**Chicago bluesman Luther
Allison, who spent much of
his career in Paris, took the
American blues scene by storm
in the mid-1990s, only to die
of cancer in 1997 at age
fifty-seven.
Chicago, 1995**

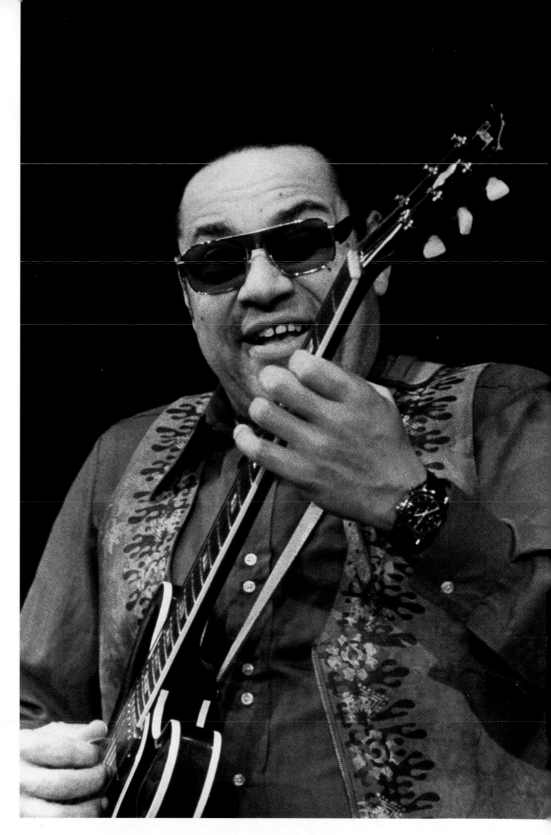

ABOVE:
**The biting guitar of Mickey Baker was featured
on countless New York recording sessions in
the 1950s, including his and Sylvia Vanderpool's
1956 smash, "Love Is Strange."
Nancy, France, 1975**

GUITARISTS

**Robben Ford started out playing with Charlie Musselwhite and Jimmy Witherspoon; he went on to work with former Beatle George Harrison and jazzman Miles Davis, among others, but kept returning to his blues roots. Oakland, California, 1997**

**"Joe Louis Walker's gospel background is evident in the healthy shake he gives his high notes." (Francis Davis, writer) San Francisco, 1997**

"Only a handful of blues harmonicists wielded as much of a lasting influence on the genre as did the sightless [Sonny] Terry [right]...who recorded some fine urban blues as a bandleader in addition to serving as guitarist Brownie McGhee's [left] longtime duet partner." (Bill Dahl, writer)
Bronx, New York, 1960

# HARMONICA PLAYERS

A DESCENDENT OF THE ANCIENT CHINESE SHENG AND COUSIN TO the harmonium, the harmonica has been known by a number of names, including mouth organ and French harp, since its invention in Thuringia, Germany, around 1820. Among blues musicians, the tiny, hand-held, lung-powered instrument has also been called the blues harp and the Mississippi saxophone.

The harmonica, in the words of Kim Field, author of *Harmonicas, Harps, and Heavy Breathers: The Evolution of the People's Instrument*, is "the most ventriloquial of musical devices." An experienced player can mimic human words such as "mama," "daddy," and "water," various wild and barnyard animal noises, and even the sounds of a locomotive chugging along the rails and blowing its whistle. These characteristics, coupled with the instrument's portability and affordability, made the harmonica ideally suited to the blues.

DeFord Bailey—a star of the Grand Ole Opry from 1925 until his forced retirement in 1941 and one of the few African-Americans to grace the Opry stage during its first half century—was a master of such techniques, as was Sonny Terry, the most famous of all country blues harmonica stylists. Born in Greensboro, Georgia, Terry was associated with singer-guitarist Blind Boy Fuller during much of the 1930s, then began an on-and-off partnership with Fuller disciple Brownie McGhee that, by the early 1960s, had sprouted into the most successful acoustic duo in blues history. Whether performing a blues or a fox-and-hound-chase routine, Terry alternated so effortlessly between high-pitched vocal wails and harmonica riffs that he often seemed to be doing both simultaneously. Terry's "mastery of the blues, his beautiful tone, and his irrepressible rhythmic drive gave him a wider range than any of his contemporaries in either the old-timey or blues camps," Field wrote.

Other notable early blues harmonica players include Jaybird Coleman, Alfred Lewis, Freeman Stowers, Hammie Nixon, as well as three who made their mark blowing with jug bands in Memphis: Will Shade of the Memphis Jug Band, Noah Lewis of Cannon's Jug Stompers, and Jed Davenport of the Beale Street Jug Band.

The harmonica has long had an especially prominent place in the Chicago blues sound. Both William "Jazz" Gillum and John Lee "Sonny Boy" Williamson recorded prolifically for RCA's Bluebird label from the mid-1930s to the late 1940s. Gillum, noted for his lively, high-end harp work, popularized such numbers as "Key to the Highway" and "Look on Yonder Wall," while Williamson was even more successful, with a string of hits that included "Good Morning Little Schoolgirl," "Early in the Morning," "Elevator Woman," and "Shake That Boogie."

Williamson was so popular that another harp blower, Aleck "Rice" Miller (who was twenty years Williamson's senior), appropriated his name and began regular broadcasts, known as *King Biscuit Time*, over radio station KFFA in Helena, Arkansas, in 1941. After John Lee's death in 1948, Miller began recording as "Sonny Boy Williamson," eventually for the

> **The Holy Grail for Chicago blowers [such as Little Walter, Carey Bell, and Junior Wells] was the harp chair in Muddy Waters's band; they measured their worth and status in terms of that seat the same way that tenor saxophonists of the swing era lusted after a slot in Count Basie's orchestra.**
> **—Kim Field,**
> **writer**

"...an other-worldly moan immediately identifies many of [Carey Bell's] more memorable harp rides." (Bill Dahl, writer) Carey Bell, shown here, at Yoshi's Jazz House with guitarist Matt Murphy. Oakland, California, 1997

Smith, George "Mojo" Buford, Paul Oscher, and Jerry Portnoy (all of whom followed Little Walter in the Waters band), as well as Billy Boy Arnold, Carey Bell, Billy Branch, Paul Butterfield, Charlie Musselwhite, and Kim Wilson. This list, of course, is only partial; a thorough accounting of Little Walter disciples could easily fill several pages.

Jimmy Reed was the most successful of the blues harp men to emerge after the release of "Juke" who managed to avoid Little Walter's awesome shadow. Blowing a rack-mounted harmonica while strumming a guitar, Reed played simple, treble-pitched squeals on his harp that ideally complemented his slurred, nasal vocal tones. This plaintive style was well received by both black and white audiences, and Reed recorded such hits for the Chicago-based Vee-Jay label as 1957's "Honest I Do" and 1960's "Baby What You Want Me to Do," both of which registered on both the R&B and pop charts. Reed's primitive approach left a pronounced mark on Louisiana bluesman Slim Harpo, who himself crossed over from R&B to pop in 1961 with "Rainin' in My Heart" and again in 1966 with "Baby Scratch My Back."

The harmonica was largely foreign to Texas-rooted California blues until George Smith settled in Los Angeles during the 1960s. By the end of the decade he was coleading a band called Bacon Fat with his young student, Rod Piazza, who went on to develop a new blues combo style with his own band, the Mighty Flyers, that fused elements of the Chicago model with earlier California jump blues. A new school of West Coast blues was born, and its leading practitioners, besides Piazza, include Rick Estrin (of Little Charlie and the Nitecats), James Harman, William Clarke, Gary Smith, Mark Hummel, Johnny Dyer, Curtis Salgado (the onetime Robert Cray Band frontman who helped inspire John Belushi and Dan Aykroyd's Blues Brothers act), and the stunningly virtuosic Paul deLay.

Checker label in Chicago, for which he scored the hits "Don't Start Me Talkin'" in 1955 and "Help Me" in 1963. Miller was even more influential than his namesake and inspired such fellow blowers as Howlin' Wolf, Little Walter, James Cotton, Junior Parker, Snooky Pryor, Paul Butterfield, and Bobby Rush.

The most famous and influential blues harmonica player of them all, however, was unquestionably Little Walter Jacobs. The Louisiana-born musician revolutionized the instrument's role in Chicago blues through his ingeniously sculpted amplified harp work as a Muddy Waters sideman and, after his instrumental number "Juke" hit the top of the R&B charts in 1952, as a leader in his own right. Little Walter was influenced by Aleck Miller and Big Walter "Shakey" Horton; Little Walter in turn influenced virtually every blues harmonica player who came after him. Some of these players include Henry Strong, Junior Wells, George

Charlie Musselwhite commented, "I just hold the harmonica and let it go. It plays itself....I think that anybody who improvises looks for that place where it [the will of the music] takes over—in all kinds of music, not just the blues. It's a universal thing. Blues and jazz are just the American versions." Sonoma, California, 1996

ABOVE:

Californian Rick Estrin is featured with Little Charlie and the Nightcats. Chicago, 1991

# SAXOPHONISTS

OTHER THAN BEING PLAYED IN JAZZ BANDS THAT ACCOMPANIED classic women blues singers of the 1920s, the saxophone did not become an integral part of the blues tradition until the 1940s. More than half a century later, some blues purists continue to view the instrument with some degree of suspicion primarily because of its associations with jazz and commercial rhythm and blues.

The musician most responsible for popularizing the saxophone in the blues context was Louis Jordan. A former member of drummer Chick Webb's jazz orchestra, the Arkansas-born saxophonist shot to stardom with his Decca recording of "I'm Gonna Move to the Outskirts of Town." His rendition of the tune, a slow blues first recorded in 1936 by its composer, Casey Bill Weldon, became one of the most popular race records of 1942. Jordan's recording spawned other successful cover versions by Big Bill Broonzy (who'd played guitar on Weldon's original), Jimmie Lunceford, and Count Basie. Jordan followed it with "I'm Gonna Leave You on the Outskirts of Town" and hit the top of *Billboard*'s black music chart (for the first of many times) later that year with the comic "What's the Use of Getting Sober." Jordan's records occupied the number one position on the magazine's black charts for a total of 101 weeks between 1942 and 1950, and more than a few of his tunes also showed up on the white charts.

Jordan's declarative vocals, into which he injected healthy doses of humor, were the primary focus of his recordings, but virtually every one featured a chorus of his biting, grit-toned saxophone (most often an alto, though he sometimes switched to tenor). These concise instrumental statements became the role models for saxophone solos in the soon-to-emerge rhythm and blues genre, for which Jordan was the primary stylistic progenitor, though his star set rapidly in the early 1950s. His unprecedented popularity during the 1940s, however, inspired a generation of musicians to pick up the saxophone.

Jordan's most obvious stylistic disciple on the alto is Earl "Good Rockin'" Brown, a California-based musician best remembered for his rippling runs on such Lowell Fulson hits of the early 1950s as "Everyday I Have the Blues" and "Blue Shadows." The prolific Hank Crawford, who first found renown as Ray Charles' musical director, also shows a pronounced Jordan influence, and Crawford in turn inspired both David Sanborn (a contemporary soul-jazz star who began his career with the Butterfield Blues Band) and James Brown sideman Maceo Parker.

Two early blues-oriented alto saxophone stars not directly affected by Jordan's approach to the instrument were Earl Bostic and Eddie "Cleanhead" Vinson. Bostic applied his stunning technical virtuosity to numerous jump blues and boogie-woogies during

> Jazz and the blues continually renewed their familial ties; most vividly, perhaps, in Illinois Jacquet's honking tenor saxophone solo on Lional Hampton's original recording of "Flyin' Home."
> —*Francis Davis,*
> **writer**

the 1940s and 1950s, but it was his syrupy renditions of popular ballads that won him the greatest acclaim. Vinson, who rose to fame as a member of Cootie Williams' band and doubled as a vocalist throughout his career, displayed a marked Charlie Parker influence in his boppish blues solos.

The tenor saxophone has, however, been the main member of the saxophone family featured in blues contexts. Some tenor men, like Big Jay McNeely, Joe Houston, Hal Singer, Red Prysock, Al Sears, and Willis "Gator Tail" Jackson, used "false" fingering along with "overblowing" techniques to produce pitches above and below the instrument's normal register; this "honking and screaming" style of instrumental rhythm and blues had its roots in the styles of Lionel Hampton sidemen Illinois Jacquet and Arnett Cobb. Other tenor players used jazz sources to create huge instrumental R&B hits of their own, as when Paul Williams turned Charlie Parker's "Now's the Time" into "The Hucklebuck" and Jimmy Forrest borrowed heavily from Duke Ellington's "Happy Go-Lucky Local" for the now standard "Night Train."

Tenor saxophone solos were regular features of R&B vocal recordings from the mid-1940s on. Among the most notable of the R&B band soloists were Buddy Floyd (with Roy Milton), Don Wilkerson (with Little Willie Littlefield and Ray Charles), Herb Hardesty (with Fats Domino), Lee Allen (with Domino and Little Richard), Dr. Wild Willie Moore (with Jimmy McCracklin), Bobby Forte (with Bobby Bland and B.B. King), and David "Fathead" Newman. The Dallas-born Newman's brilliantly sculpted, bop-tinged tenor (and sometimes alto) statements were highlights of numerous Ray Charles records cut between 1954 and 1964; in subsequent years Newman made significant contributions to sessions by such artists as B.B. King, Dr. John, and Lou Rawls, and recorded a series of jazz albums of

his own. Other jazz tenor players who cut their teeth in blues-oriented bands include John Coltrane (with both Eddie Vinson and Earl Bostic) and Stanley Turrentine (with Lowell Fulson and Bostic).

Sam "The Man" Taylor, Cab Calloway's star tenor soloist in the 1940s, dominated the New York recording studio scene during the 1950s, playing in R&B and rock and roll sessions until he was supplanted in 1958 by the even-more-versatile King Curtis. Born in Fort Worth, Texas, saxophonist and occasional blues singer Curtis lent his distinctive blues tenor touch to nearly everyone—from the Coasters and Bobby Darin to Aretha Franklin and John Lennon—who passed through the Big Apple over the next thirteen years. The beneficiaries of his efforts include such blues artists as Chuck Willis, Roosevelt Sykes, Champion Jack Dupree, and Esther Phillips. Playing similar roles in Los Angeles studios were Maxwell Davis and Plas Johnson.

Saxophones were largely missing from Chicago blues bands, the ensemble role filled instead by harmonicas. Noteworthy exceptions include tenor saxophonists J.T. Brown (best known for his work with Elmore James), Eddie Shaw (with Howlin' Wolf), and A.C. Reed (with Buddy Guy and Junior Wells).

Among significant tenor players who blew onto the international blues scene during the 1980s and 1990s are Johnny Nocturne Band leader John Firmin, former Roomful of Blues frontman Greg Piccolo, and Austin-based musician Mark "Kaz" Kazanoff.

**OPPOSITE:**
**Tenorman Illinois Jacquet starred with the Lionel Hampton and Count Basie bands and was the ultimate crowd-pleaser at Jazz at the Philharmonic concerts. Boston, 1966**

**BELOW:**
**"[Johnny] Hodges was an undisputed master of both the blues and the romantic ballad, a combination of talents less common than one might guess." (Tom Piazza, writer) Boston, 1958**

"Hank Crawford's records are swinging parties built on the blues, Southern R&B and enough bebop to keep a hardened jazz listener involved."
(Richard Cook and Brian Morton, writers)
Boston, 1965

ABOVE:
Texas saxophonist King Curtis was a top New York R&B session player in the 1950s and 1960s.
Boston, 1966

RIGHT:
"[David 'Fathead' Newman's] logical solos in the middle of Ray Charles' tunes made me see the beauty of ad-libbing. I heard melody inside his improvisations."
(Joel Dorn, record producer)
Boston, 1965

# PIANISTS

OPPOSITE:

**"Otis Spann, a subtle and unobtrusive pianist, but one also capable of a thunderous boogie woogie reminiscent of Big Maceo." (Giles Oakley, writer) Boston, 1966**

OTIS SPANN'S FINGERS MAY HAVE BEEN STUBBY, BUT HE PLAYED more piano than anybody else on the Chicago blues scene during the 1950s and 1960s and was considered by many to have been the best since Big Maceo Merriweather. The Mississippi-born musician added just the right two-handed touch—sometimes aggressive, other times understated—to recordings by such artists as Little Walter, Aleck "Sonny Boy Williamson" Miller, Howlin' Wolf, Chuck Berry, Bo Diddley, Buddy Guy, and John Lee Hooker. It was as the anchor of the Muddy Waters band from 1953 to 1969, however, that Spann made his greatest contributions. Spann and Waters claimed to have been half-brothers, though they weren't. They were, nevertheless, kindred spirits, and Spann knew Waters' music better than any other musician, supplying a rhythmically propulsive foundation of rock-solid bass patterns and complex treble figures that wove effortlessly in and around—and, at times, anticipated—Waters' and other soloist's lines.

> Veterans of the work camps and barrelhouses [like] Memphis Slim, Champion Jack Dupree, Roosevelt Sykes and Sunnyland Slim didn't "tickle" the keys.... They crushed them. The trick was to make yourself heard....Play and sing loud.
> —*Francis Davis,*
> **writer**

Singing in a soulful, gin-soaked drawl, Spann cut a number of albums of his own during the 1960s and, though none were huge sellers, built up enough of a reputation on the blues circuit to break away from Waters in 1969 and try a solo career. The pianist was diagnosed with cancer the following year, however, and didn't live long enough to see "Hungry Country Girl," a single he'd cut the previous year with Fleetwood Mac, become a jukebox hit in blues bars across the United States. Spann died just one month after his fortieth birthday.

From the 1920s to the present, the Windy City has seen more than its share of great blues piano players. While such jazz-oriented pianists as Lovie Austin, Lillian Hardin Armstrong, and Thomas A. Dorsey regularly provided accompaniment for classic blues singers in Chicago studios during the 1920s, a rougher strain known as barrelhouse took hold in the 1930s and 1940s with the arrival of players from the South like Little Brother Montgomery, Blind John Davis, Memphis Slim, Roosevelt Sykes, Eddie Boyd, Sunnyland Slim, and Big Maceo Merriweather. Maceo's 1941 waxing of "Worried Life Blues" ranks as one of the most influential blues piano recordings of all time (Ray Charles cut a remarkable version of it on electric piano in 1960). Many of these men continued playing into the electric blues era and were joined by such others as Little Johnny Jones, Willie Mabon, Lafayette Leake, Mark Naftalin, and Joe Willie "Pinetop" Perkins. Of the major Chicago blues pianists, only Alfonzo "Sonny" Thompson (who is best remembered for his late-1940s instrumental hits "Long Gone" and "Late Freight" and for his later studio work with Lula Reed and Freddie King) was born there.

One-time boxer Champion Jack Dupree was among the first generation of New Orleans barrelhouse stylists to achieve national fame. Dupree's 1941 recording of "Junker's Blues" served as the model for the 1949 debut of "The Fat Man," Antoine "Fats" Domino,

the most famous Crescent City piano pumper of them all. Fats Domino also adapted the steady triplet piano style pioneered by Texas-born, California-based bluesman Little Willie Littlefield for such subesquent hits as "Goin' Home" and "Goin' to the River." If Domino had the greatest national success, rising from his barrelhouse roots to become an icon of early rock and roll, Roy "Professor Longhair" Byrd had the most lasting impact on fellow New Orleans pianists. Among the many disciples of Byrd's highly syncopated "rhumba boogie" approach are Allen Toussaint, Huey "Piano" Smith, Dr. John, and Henry Butler. Other notable New Orleans blues pianists include Tuts Washington, Archibald, and the awesome James Booker.

A California school of blues piano emerged during World War II, spearheaded in Los Angeles by Charles Brown and in Oakland by Ivory Joe Hunter. Both were recent arrivals from Texas and brought a sophisticated, jazz-rooted sensibility to the blues. Other Texas piano players who launched their careers in the Golden State were Little Willie Littlefield, Amos Milburn, Camille Howard, Floyd Dixon, Lloyd Glenn, and Omar Sharriff. Glenn was the only one of the bunch who didn't sing; he found success as an instrumentalist, scoring such hits as "Old Time Shuffle Blues" and "Chica Boo," as well contributing his rippling arpeggios to record dates by T-Bone Walker, Lowell Fulson, B.B. King, and others. Of the non-Texans who made their marks as pianists on the

**Little Willie Littlefield is a superb blues and boogie-woogie stylist. Chicago, 1986**

California blues scene, Cecil Gant, Jimmy McCracklin, and Ray Charles are particulary noteworthy.

Other important blues piano stylists who don't fit handily into the Texas-to-California, Mississippi-to-Chicago, or New Orleans schemes include Sammy Price, a Texas-born New York studio musician who spent nearly half a century backing a wide variety of artists, from blues singers Georgia White, Joe Turner, and Dr. Horse to gospel singers Sister Rosetta Tharpe and Marie Knight to jazz instrumentalists Lester Young and Sidney Bechet; Mississsippi-born Ike Turner, who played piano for Howlin' Wolf and B.B. King, among others, before taking up the guitar and Tina Turner; the West Virginia-born, St. Louis-based Johnnie Johnson, whose rollicking two-fisted attack propelled Chuck Berry on such seminal rock and roll hits as "Maybellene," "Roll Over Beethhoven," and "School Day"; and Ray Bryant, the most deeply blues-influenced jazz pianist of the bop generation.

Boogie-woogie, of course, was the most popular strain of blues piano. Marked by a steady eight-to-the-bar pattern played with the left hand, the style was pioneered in the 1920s by such players as Cow Cow Davenport, Meade "Lux" Lewis, Jimmy Yancey, and Clarence "Pinetop" Smith. It was, in fact, Smith's 1928 recording of "Pinetop's Boogie Woogie" that gave the genre its name. Boogie-woogie became a fad in the late 1930s and early 1940s, and Lewis became a national attraction, along with such other players as Albert Ammons, Pete Johnson, and Freddie Slack. At the height of the boogie-woogie craze, the style often got divorced from its blues roots, with some pianists even working up boogie treatments of European classical themes. Boogie-woogie faded from the popular consciousness at the end of the 1940s, although its distinct rhythms continue to be felt throughout the world of blues piano as a whole.

"Memphis Slim was worshiped in Paris as a blues demigod.... His height and regal bearing adding to the drama of his slow, atmospheric piano blues." (Francis Davis, writer)
Paris, 1968

ABOVE:

"A good-natured bear of a man who combined a powerful voice and piano style...Roosevelt Sykes was nicknamed 'The Honeydripper' in honor of his way with women." (Francis Davis, writer) Englewood Cliffs, New Jersey, 1960

OPPOSITE:

A one-time boxer, pianist Champion Jack Dupree was very popular with European audiences. Paris, 1961

TOP LEFT:
"Texas-born Sammy Price was the only blues pianist of his generation whose work showed a keen sense of jazz harmony." (Francis Davis, writer) Bern, Switzerland, 1987

BOTTOM LEFT:
The exceptional singer-pianist James Booker would fill a set with complex boogies, New Orleans shuffles, ragtime, and even classical pieces. New Orleans, 1976

ABOVE:
Pianist, record producer, and song-writer Allen Toussaint was greatly influenced by Roy "Professor Longhair" Byrd. Newport, Rhode Island, 1996

Swamp blues piano
queen Katie Webster.
Chicago, 1994

# INDEX

## PHOTOGRAPHY CREDITS